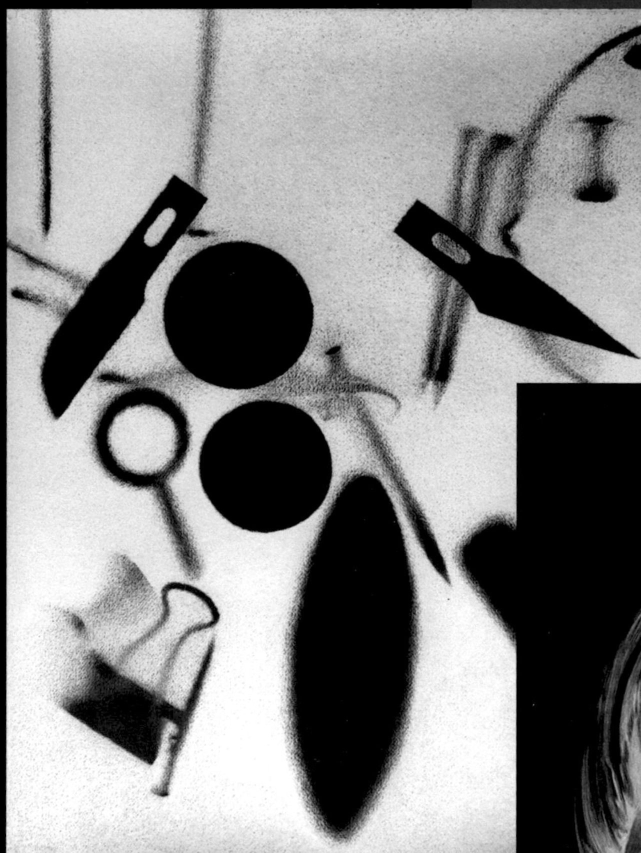

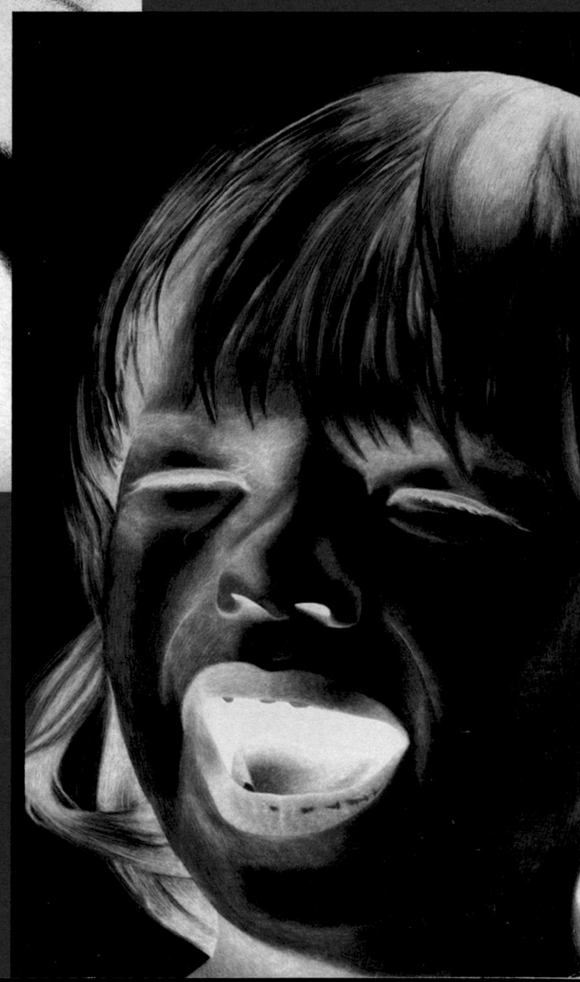

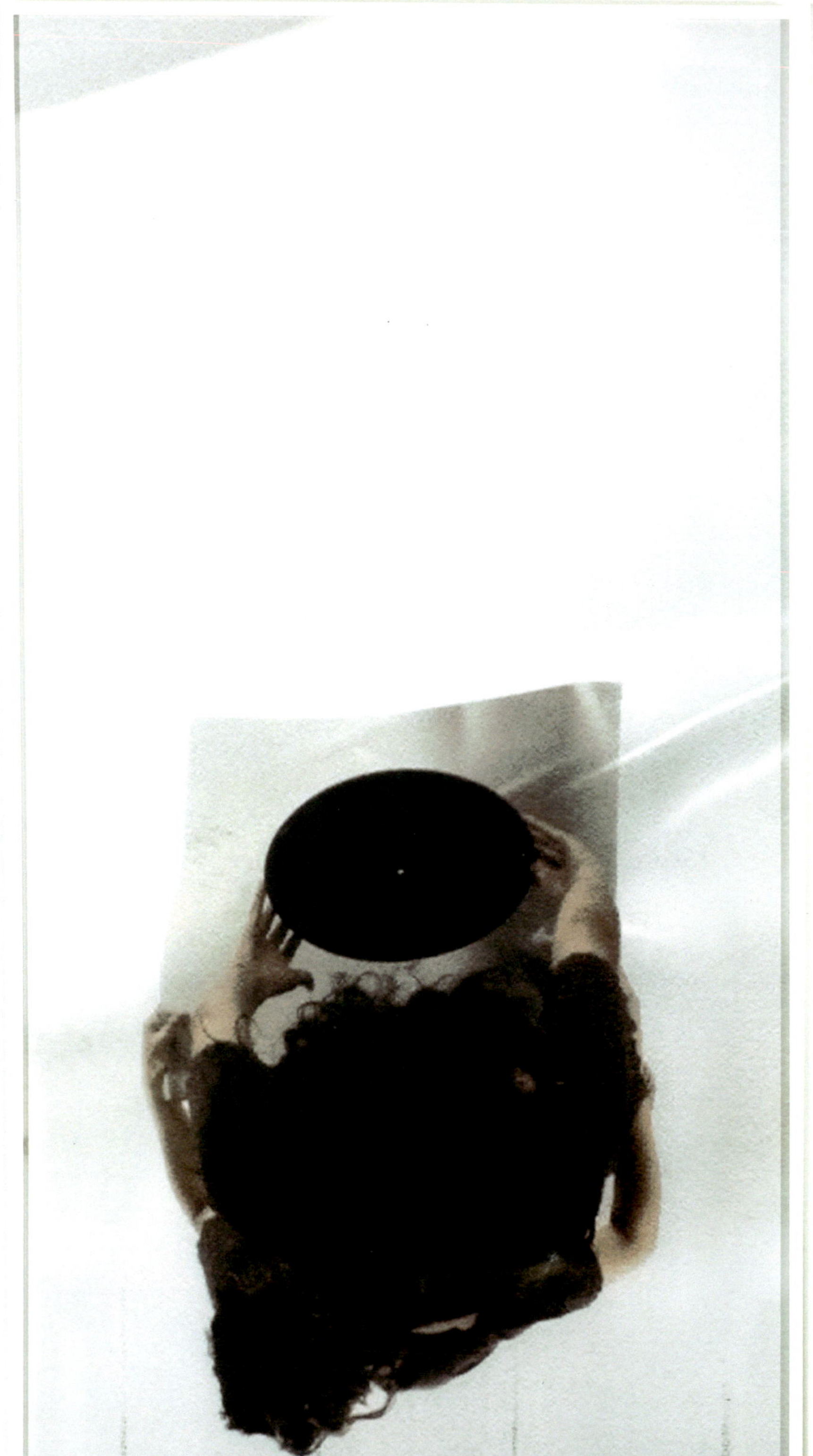

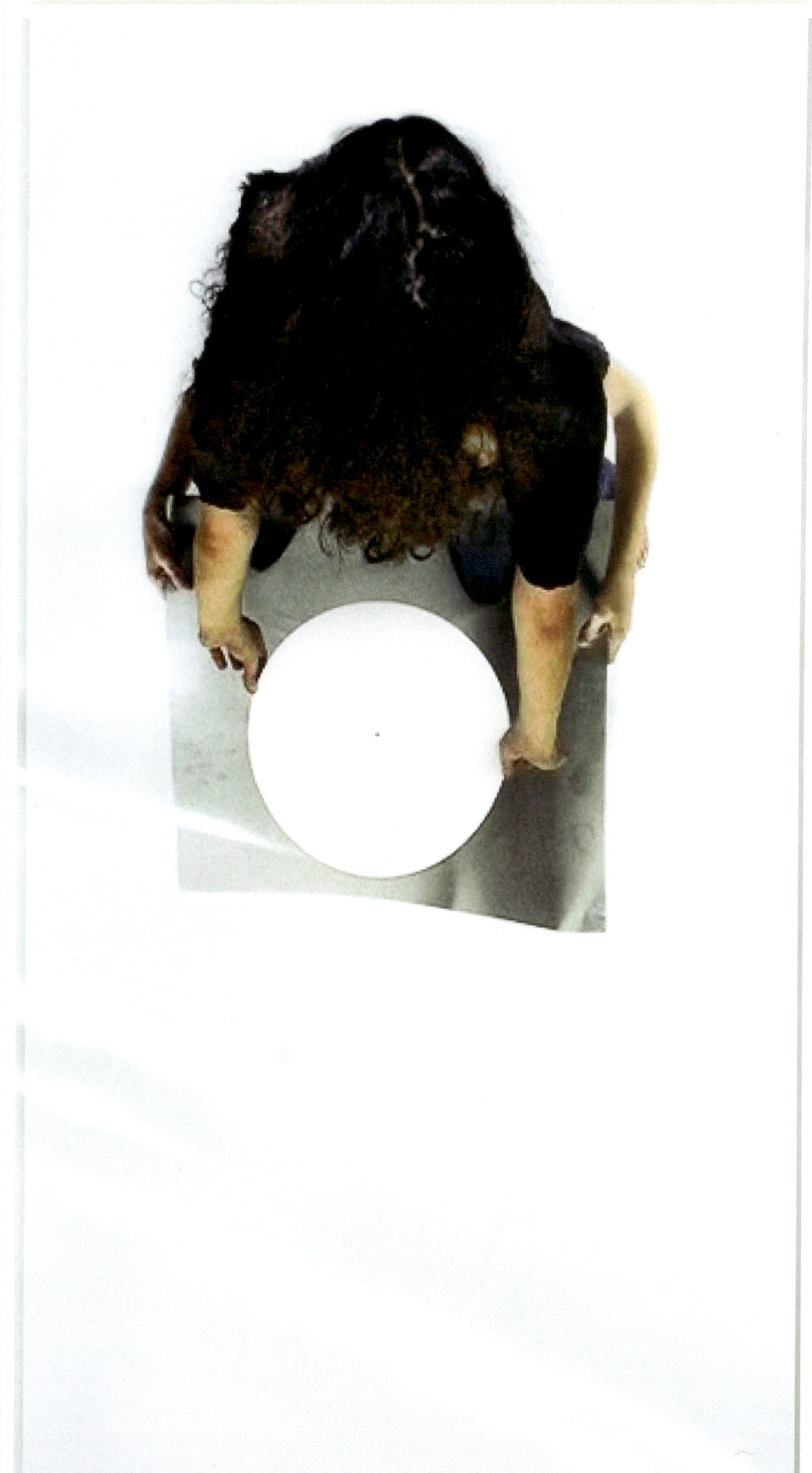

Image Transfer: Pictures in a Remix Culture
Published in conjunction with the exhibition *Image Transfer: Pictures in a Remix Culture* held at the Henry Art Gallery, University of Washington from October 2, 2010 to January 23, 2011. Exhibition tour coordinated by Independent Curators International.

Includes biographical references.

ISBN 978-0-935558-49-4
Designed by Gabriel Stromberg
Printed in Canada by Hemlock Printers Ltd.

Image Transfer: Pictures in a Remix Culture is curated by Sara Krajewski and is a traveling exhibition co-organized by the Henry Art Gallery and Independent Curators International (ICI), New York, and circulated by ICI. The Presenting Sponsor for this exhibition is The Boeing Company. Additional support is provided by the Paul G. Allen Family Foundation, ArtsFund, 4Culture/King County Lodging Tax, and the Seattle Office of Arts & Cultural Affairs. Support to ICI for the exhibition and tour is provided by The Horace W. Goldsmith Foundation, The Andy Warhol Foundation for the Visual Arts, The Cowles Charitable Trust, the ICI Board of Trustees, and ICI Benefactors Barbara and John Robinson.

Independent Curators International (ICI) produces exhibitions, events, publications, and training opportunities for diverse audiences around the world. A catalyst for independent thinking, ICI connects emerging and established curators, artists, and institutions, to forge international networks and generate new forms of collaboration. Working across disciplines and historical precedents, the organization is a hub that provides access to the people, ideas, and practices that are key to current developments in the field, inspiring fresh ways of seeing and contextualizing contemporary art.

cover:
Sean Dack
Wing (Economy Class). 2006
Chromogenic print

inside spread:
Karl Haendel
Image courtesy of the artist

previous spread:
Erika Vogt
I arrive when I am foreign (Record No Record). 2007
Lightjet Type-C Prints

following page:
Carter Mull
Spilling, New York Times May 7, 2010. 2010
Ink on paper

iCI

IMAGE TRANSFER
PICTURES IN A REMIX CULTURE

Sara Krajewski

Henry Art Gallery
University of Washington, Seattle

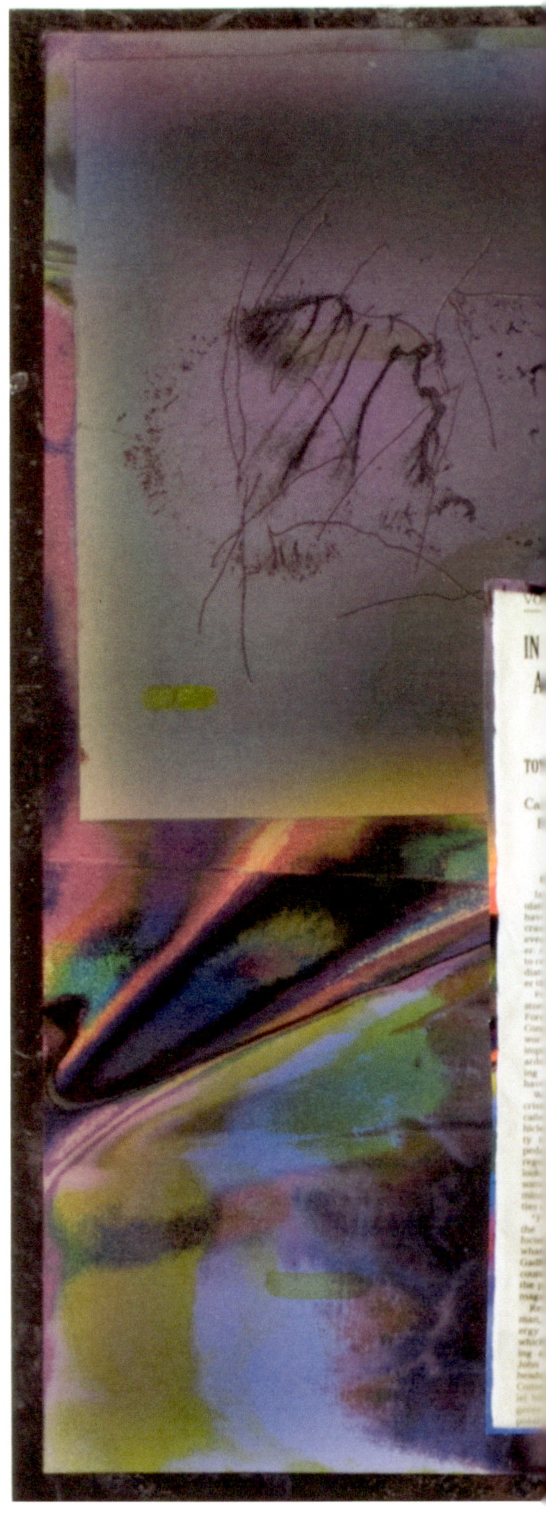

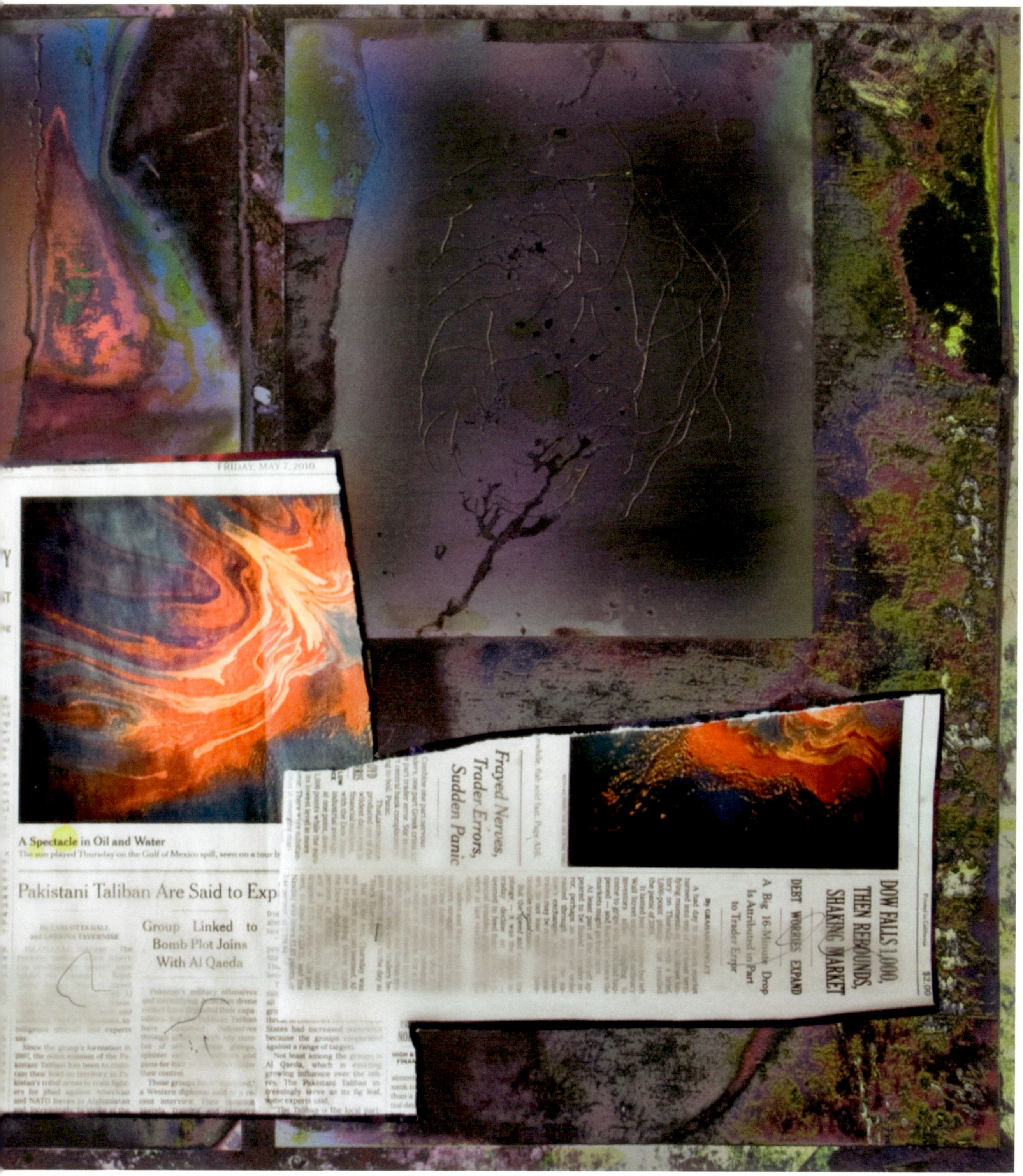
FRIDAY, MAY 7, 2010
A Spectacle in Oil and Water
The sun played Thursday on the Gulf of Mexico spill, seen on a tour b
Pakistani Taliban Are Said to Exp
Group Linked to Bomb Plot Joins With Al Qaeda
DOW FALLS 1,000, THEN REBOUNDS, SHAKING MARKET
DEBT WORRIES EXPAND
A Big 16-Minute Drop Is Attributed in Part to Trader Error
Frayed Nerves, Trader Errors, Sudden Panic
$2.00

CONTENTS

Foreword

From European collagists in the early 1900s to contemporary installation artists who cull elements from the garbage bin and the Internet, the recycling of materials and ideas has been a fertile practice in modern and contemporary art. Indeed, the fragmentation of elements as seen in Cubist collage, montage, Pop Art, Assemblage, and Appropriation has led to the alteration of aesthetic systems of order. This, in turn, has affected how artists make art, how the public absorbs photographic images, and how critical theorists understand, interpret, and decode visual culture. *Image Transfer: Pictures in a Remix Culture* examines the work of twelve artists who transfer images from one context, physical configuration, or presentation platform to another in an effort to evaluate and question what curator Sara Krajewski calls "the dynamic spectacle of the information age."

That spirit of inquiry is in keeping with The Henry Art Gallery's eighty-three-year history of innovation. The Henry has long championed art by painters, sculptors, and performance artists who use the camera as a tool of creative expression. As a result, photography is a core strength of our collection of more than 25,000 objects. I am indebted to Sara Krajewski, the organizer of the exhibition and author of this book, for viewing hundreds of artists' work over two years time and making a selection that is both rich and broad in scope. Her keen eye and astute judgment have given shape to a complex aspect of contemporary art.

With heartfelt thanks I also wish to acknowledge The Boeing Company, Presenting Sponsor for this project. Additional support is provided by the Paul G. Allen Family Foundation, ArtsFund, 4Culture/King County Lodging Tax, and the Seattle Office of Arts & Cultural Affairs. Finally, I join Sara Krajewski in thanking the artists featured in this book for sharing their thoughts, and for bringing us to a greater awareness of our multi-faceted world through their art.

Sylvia Wolf
Director, Henry Art Gallery

Acknowledgements

Image Transfer: Pictures in a Remix Culture is the culmination of two years of looking at, thinking about, and discussing developments in contemporary photographic practice. Initially attracted to the trends toward abstraction and materialist approaches to the medium, I shifted my focus towards the proliferation of extant photographic images appearing in other works of art—as points of content, formal devices, material objects, and sites of process. This exhibition continues my interest in how photography structures our visual culture and affects our ways of seeing the world, perspectives I have also explored in other exhibitions for the Henry Art Gallery: *Seeing the Unseen* (2005) and *Viewfinder* (2007).

As this exhibition took shape, many friends and colleagues offered thoughts, advice, and insight. I am thankful for all the conversations with Jeff Fisher, Laurel Gitlen, David Hartt, Alex Klein, Carter Mull, Lisa Oppenheim, Shaw Osha, Vesna Pavlovic, Margot Quan Knight, and John Tevis. From concept to final installation, Henry Chief Curator Elizabeth Brown has been a wonderful sounding board, devil's advocate, and tireless supporter. I am grateful to Henry Director Sylvia Wolf who offered attentive guidance as I refined the exhibition's content. A special thanks to Sylvia and Liz for pushing me to expand my notion of what this show could be and the audiences it could reach.

The incredibly talented and dedicated Henry staff transforms ideas, checklists, and floor plans into stellar exhibitions, publications, and programs. Exhibitions Manager Paul Cabarga coordinated the countless details of loans, contracts, and budgets; his scrupulous editing whipped the catalogue into shape. Former Curatorial Associate Misa Jeffereis offered invaluable assistance with coordinating materials for the publication and the exhibition's installation, assisted by Rachel Gaudry, curatorial work study student. University of Washington art history graduate students Jennifer Beetem and Kimberly Hereford were indispensible research assistants. Jim Rittimann, Exhibition Designer and Head Preparator, along with preparators Dan Gurney and Eric Adami, provided important technical expertise and installed the exhibition beautifully. I am indebted to the distinctive sensibility of Gabriel Stromberg, who designed this lovely publication.

This exhibition would not have been possible without the help of several people working on behalf of the participating artists: Anthony Allen, Paula Cooper

Gallery; Chris Perez, Ratio 3; Jessie Washburne-Harris, Harris Lieberman Gallery; Susanne Vielmetter and Sasha Drosdick, Susanne Vielmetter Los Angeles Projects; Bridget Donahue formerly of D'Amelio Terras; Claudia Altman-Siegel, Altman Siegel Gallery; Kristina Kite, Overduin and Kite; Marc Foxx and Rodney Hill, Marc Foxx Gallery; Richard Arregui, Frederic Snitzer Gallery; Loring Randolph, Casey Kaplan; Josie Browne, Max Protetch Gallery; and Mary Leigh Cherry and Philip Martin, Cherry and Martin. In addition to the artists and galleries who lent work to the exhibition, I would like to thank the private individuals who generously loaned art from their collections: Robert Harshorn Shimshak and Marion Brenner, the Miller Meigs Collection, Dr. Paul Marks, the Piper Family Collection, Kelly and Jeff Poe, John Rubeli, Helen and Charles Schwab, and a number of anonymous private donors. Special recognition to Artist Pension Trust for lending as well.

The exhibition's tour was ably coordinated by Independent Curators International. A warm thanks to Kate Fowle, Executive Director, Renaud Proch, Deputy Director, Susan Hapgood, Senior Advisor, and Fran Wu Giarratano, Exhibitions Manager for backing my vision and enabling many more viewers from across the country to experience this exhibition.

It was a great honor and pleasure to work with the twelve artists included in *Image Transfer*—Sean Dack, Karl Haendel, Jordan Kantor, Matt Keegan, Carter Mull, Lisa Oppenheim, Marlo Pascual, Amanda Ross-Ho, Sara VanDerBeek, Siebren Versteeg, Erika Vogt, and Kelley Walker. It is incredibly vitalizing to engage with this many artists working at the top of their game, responding deeply and individually to the exhibition's topic, my ideas, and the work of their peers. This experience has been deeply rewarding for me. Thank you!

Sara Krajewski
Associate Curator, Henry Art Gallery

Moving Images

Sara Krajewski

We live in a truly raucous visual culture. A constantly changing, overcrowded field of vision—animated by the Internet, social media, video games, television, movies, glossy magazines, and countless other virtual and real experiences—floods our awareness. Though we have a hand in populating, and then perpetuating this universe, images break away from us (as their creators and viewers), shaking off their original context and moving freely from screen to screen, eyeball to eyeball. These virally circulating free agents of visual language wield an ability to influence perception, collapse time and distance, trigger reaction, and hold sway over our psyches, much to the chagrin of logic.

This dynamic spectacle of the information age is alluring. Because of the speed with which media images come at us, it is difficult to pause and think about how the image's role as a "mobile sign"[1] affects us. Many artists, as critical image producers and consumers, react to this all-encompassing world by adopting and adapting from its myriad sources. Photographic images culled from websites, printed matter, television, film, personal and public archives, from studio walls, and

1 Lev Manovich, *The Language of New Media*, (Cambridge, MA: The MIT Press, 2001), xxii. Manovich speaks to this concept throughout his introductory "Prologue: Vertov's Dataset."

from other works of art are all fair game. Artists divert these readily transformable visual materials into new territories of formal and idiomatic expression. An image lifted from one site may be embedded in another composition. It may be altered through various procedures or remade through copying. The processes of image transfer could even be considered a decentralized mode of photography where the use of a camera is but one application in building an image synthesized from other images.

The activity of image transfer has been with us throughout art history. Modern permutations can be traced through Cubist and Dada collages, Pop silkscreens, the technique of superimposition in experimental film, and the appropriation of the "Pictures" generation of artists. This multifaceted practice has shaped a range of concerns from formal experimentation to political commentary. Critical statements arise from direct juxtapositions, jarring context shifts, bald repetition, and other tactics. Now, more images on more media platforms seen by more people bring further opportunities for studied engagement. An image transfer strategy takes on a new vitality for contemporary artists driven to examine the changeable appearance and meaning of images. Whether artists delve into an image's semiotic properties, or its ability to enchant, or its material manifestation, their attitudes and approaches to repurposing pictures reflect a fluent rethinking of the way we value images today.

Photographic images still function today as documents and mementos in the classic sense. But because they are more readily detached from their origins and subjected to a large variety of processes, they function more and more like collage elements waiting to be repositioned. After seeing an online joke that photoshopped Bert (from public television's Sesame Street) and Osama bin Laden onto a poster at an insurgent rally, artist Charlie White deemed that "the image's potential for total transmutability became abundantly clear."[2] With a few clicks of a mouse to execute "cut" and "paste" commands, you can make for yourself an al-Qaeda Muppet. It is now commonplace to see authenticity dislodged when unexpected associations are made for the sake of affective impact.

Strategies of redirecting, recombining, repurposing, and remixing loaded visual materials pervade the creative fields of our day. After all, ours is a remix culture, where the phenomena of collage, montage, superimposition, mash-ups, loops, and quick edits are now primary forms in music, TV, film and video, visual art, and literature.[3] Technology powerfully amplifies the availability and sophistication of these techniques. The use of computer software to sample, copy, fragment, alter, and distribute has become second nature for many, artist or not. Growing alongside remix practices, the popular advocacy of free culture, open source, and copyleft turn the traditional notions of intellectual property, authorship, and copyright on end. In this climate, it is not surprising that current artistic practices consider images to be unencumbered bits of information ready to be plugged into new contexts.

Remix is a term most quickly associated with popular music and DJ culture. The history of recorded music is the domain of a DJ. But, for the DJ that history is not linear, rather it resembles a network of "mobile segments" ready to be combined and inscribed into new compositions and mixes.[4] DJs approach the breadth of source materials as if they were accessing and implementing digital information—cutting, layering, and ordering seemingly random elements to form sonic collages. Nicolas Bourriaud observes that the "work of the DJ consists in conceiving linkages through which works flow into each other representing at once a product, a tool, and a medium."[5] No specific style is mandatory, but technique and technology remain consistent across stylistic vocabularies. Image transfer art correlates with this musical practice. Distinguished by its methods, it is not necessarily defined by its content. Importantly, it envelopes many artistic intentions and is not limited to any one conceptual agenda.

Musical remix came about through the culture of recording, a culture that enabled songs and compositions to circulate free from the specific time and place of performance.[6] The ubiquitous use of instant cameras, and now digital ones, marks a similar moment in visual culture when a first-hand observation could be captured by an individual and shared immediately. Everyone can play with a camera—the labor of making images is entirely automated, allowing us to take a lot of them quickly and easily. Vilém Flusser designates this current of "technical images" as forceful and irresistible: "there is no artistic, scientific or political activity which is not aimed at it, there is no everyday activity which does not aspire to be photographed, filmed, video-taped... for there is a general desire

---

2 Charlie White, "Cut and Paste: The Collage Impulse Today," *Artforum*, Vol. XLVII, No. 7 (March 2009): 212. See www.bertisevil.tv.

3 Lawrence Lessig, "Free(ing) Culture for Remix," *Utah Law Review*, Vol. 2004, Issue 4 (2004): 965.

4 Christoph Cox and Daniel Warner, eds., *Audio Culture: Readings in Modern Music*, (New York: Continuum, 2004), 330.

5 Nicolas Bourriaud, *Postproduction*, (New York: Lukas & Sternberg, 2002), 40.

6 Cox and Warner, 329.

to be endlessly remembered and endlessly repeatable."[7]

According to Flusser's argument, the camera is the central apparatus of the "photographic program," in the service of elite political and corporate industrial powers. Photographers succumb to this program and their continuous activity subtracts from a seemingly inexhaustible array of actual views to enrich the powerful photographic universe one image at a time.[8] Ultimately, for the photographer and photographic practice to break out of this constantly evolving, self-perpetuating program, something "human" must be inserted into the technological core. The "experimental photographer is consciously attempting to create unpredictable information, i.e. to release themselves from the camera and to place within the image something that is not in its program. They know they are playing against the camera."[9]

At the moment, questions about the future of the photographic medium are causing widespread debate and artists are exercising a particularly free license to reconsider photography's roles and methods. This wide and deep reevaluation has given rise to an array of media-based image creation strategies and philosophies. Often utilizing a camera and related tools, these artists redirect the image's current capacity to be utterly detached from context in ways that challenge the programmatic exploitation of this mobility of meaning.

For those who tap into a nearly limitless range of source materials there is an enormous range of processes with which to move these images into, around, or through their work. Downloading digital content, scanning and uploading analog images, and executing the commands of editing and imaging software are a given. In an online environment where jpegs, tiffs, and video files circulate widely and with ease, an attitude that favors the free use of anything one finds prevails, even if the thing one finds is a picture in a book or an archive.

Technology is only part of the equation, however. To a great degree it has influenced our behavior, but it hasn't yet totally transformed how we make art and images and how we consume them. In contemporary art the physicality of objects, even the appropriated photograph as a thing, still manages to stave off digital dematerialization—for now. Participation in both the digital and the analog world amounts to a promising wealth of possibilities for both content and process. Going outside the predominant cultural trend, the presence of the object is essential for many contemporary artists: a strong connection to materials as well as the evidence of the hand, holds fast. Many continue to use conventional techniques of cut-and-paste, staged photography, and other object-oriented studio practices as they construct new images, objects, and situations. Yet at the core, image transfer artists engage the use of extant photo-based images as material building blocks for their work. Like the DJ's mix, this strategic move places the floating sample into a new chain of signification.[10] From here, their options are nearly unlimited.

Taking a brief look at three distinct approaches will help ground us in this open field and function as a conceptual or practical map that stakes out the reach of this ever more present artistic practice.[11] Each example that follows engages with essential elements underlying the mobility of signs—language, time, and context—yet does so with a unique perspective that serves to expand the critical discourse around the gripping vibrancy of our visual culture.

Many image transfer artists situate their work in relationship to their predecessors by building upon historical uses of appropriation that critiqued the use of the image as a tool for establishing and perpetuating social hierarchies. Artists like Lisa Oppenheim examine how images are presented and distributed for the purpose of communicating or reinstating certain beliefs or values. Oppenheim also considers how changes in context and the passage of time affect the interpretation of a given photograph. Choosing images from archives as varied as the Library of Congress, *Life* magazine, and Flickr.com, she might rephotograph the source materials or send them through various reproductive processes like photocopying. The image is either reconstituted and re-viewed, or it is degraded. Oppenheim's methods literally and metaphorically embody how time's passage and the image's insertion into new contexts affect its past and present meanings. The works comment upon the past, as well as current, perceptions of the subject.

Approaches such as Oppenheim's raise questions about mobile signs: Does anything have a fixed meaning or context today? If an image is truly fluid how is it that it still communicates something to us? A consensus of shared meaning must exist, otherwise the image cannot function as an element of visual language. With everything open to interpretation, manipulation, and relocation, some artists find it imperative to work at connecting mobile signs to meaning, whether it is the orig-

---

7 Vilém Flusser, *Towards a Philosophy of Photography*, (London: Reaktion Books, 2000), 20.

8 Flusser, 26.

9 Flusser, 81.

10 Cox and Warner, 330.

11 Jerry Saltz, "Great Artists Steal," Artnet Magazine, May 18, 2009, http://www.artnet.com/magazineus/features/saltz/saltz5-18-09.asp. Saltz likened the current proliferation of appropriation to "esthetic kudzu."

inally intended one or one that has been assigned through shifts in cultural values.

In other approaches to this transportability of meaning, artists assemble several pictures as formal and linguistic elements in collage-like compositions. Here images function syntactically—several inserted into one frame relate to each other like parts of a sentence. Shuffling these pictorial signs and playing off their original content elicits thoughts and reactions from the viewer as a reader or interpreter. These forays into creatively deploying visual language function on a cognitive level as we are asked to make sense of varied, often disjointed, visual data. Moving from the concrete to the abstract, they also operate phenomenologically, forming mindful investigations into sensory experience.

For the basis of his recent large-scale photographs, Carter Mull opens newspaper spreads so that ads butt up against news photos and snapshots he has attached to the surface of the final print. Desire, documentation, and memory seem to jostle within the picture plane, vying for our attention: a familiar sensation many of us have when looking at our networked data screens full of similar fleeting visual stimuli. Mull's investigation into our consumption of visual information collects and manipulates the technical images Flusser identified (snapshots, news photos, etc.) by using the readily available tools of image production (consumer-grade digital camera and Photoshop software). Pushing the mundane to great lengths, Mull's images form open-ended reflections only resolved for viewers through their own individual perceptual, emotional, or analytical connection to the various, often loaded, materials the artist presents.

Combining multiple images into a single frame also collapses the comprehension of a photograph as a record of a distinct time and place. This shift away from the perception of a frozen moment allows an expanded relationship or even a narrative to emanate from these layers. New media theorist Lev Manovich identifies a technique of avant garde film that offers a parallel: the superimposition of images and multiple screens that result in a montage within a single shot. Separate realities form contingent parts of a single image.[12] Multiple moments of time join up within the frame.

This is precisely the experience explored by Erika Vogt when she composes layers of still photographs and moving projections one upon another. For a series of photographs from 2006, Vogt performed with distinctive props in front of photographed images of herself holding those exact props. Her actions were captured on video but then printed as stills. The final, life-size photographs create temporally layered self-portraits containing multiple, strangely un-mirror-like images. Here, linear perspective is skewed in favor of a set of spatial relationships, not sequential ones, that establish a narrative situation. Vogt's approach to superimposition is distinctively live and performative, taking place in the studio space rather than on a flattened screen in an editing suite. In this setting, she stretches her use of the camera beyond its normal functions, subjecting an image or device to another image or device's rules of engagement: a still image becomes animate and a video camera produces a static portrait, for example. Vogt is not alone in the creative misapplication of technology to achieve unusual imaging effects. Among the tools used for image transfer, working against the grain of one's equipment is enabling new visualizations of how we experience time and perceive our world.

What characterizes the various image transfer practices is a broad consideration of an image as visual data linked to a time and a place but not bound to either one specifically. To attempt to better situate this paradoxically definitive-yet-indefinite condition, a recent essay by Jan Verwoert on reconsidering appropriation may provide a speculative framework for contextualizing this wide-ranging artistic practice.

Verwoert proposes that, "the challenge of the moment is ... to re-think the meaning of appropriation in relation to a reality constituted by a multiplicity of spatialized temporalities."[13] Technology and globalization in contemporary life team up to create a sense of many localized strands, even loops, of time. (We are not all on the same teleological path of history.) Appropriation—particularly the reuse of images—can speak to multiple and interconnected conceptions of time/location. Its outcomes enact a view of time and place occupying cycles that give shape to simultaneous and/or fractured states of being.

Verwoert further states that, "the object of appropriation ... must today be made to speak not only of its place within the structural order of the present material culture but also of the different times it inhabits and the different historical vectors that cross it."[14] In Verwoert's formulation the effect of the dominant postmodern theoretical position of the last 30 years designated appropriated objects or images as "dead signs," condemned to a single reading often set in a political context of institutional critique. In sharp contrast, the mobility of image signs today obliges us to see them operating in a wide-open field of interpretation and use. To consider

---

12 Manovich, xvii.

13 Jan Verwoert, "Apropos Appropriation: Why stealing images today feels different," *Art & Research*, vol. 1, no. 2 (Summer 2007), http://www.artandresearch.org.uk/v1n2/verwoert.html.

14 Verwoert, n.p.

an image crossing time and space necessitates questions. How did its trajectory come to assign a particular meaning at a given moment? How will another repositioning further activate and complicate the image's associations and the contexts in which it appears? This expressive potential is what moves the current generation of artists to propose new roles for these active agents.

An important word for Verwoert is "invocation"—as if appropriated objects and images could conjure up echoes of their previous significance that now haunt their present incarnation. Rather than take a passive position, say, to depict or document, the recycled image is active and continues to resonate. Such action words also suggest that we reconsider appropriative strategies as time-based ones. This status fits remix culture. Images are not static; artists interact with these empowered entities and build new art experiences influenced by their dynamic nature.

As we grapple with the potential for the photograph to be something more than a captured depiction, what impact do these images as mobile signs have on the medium of photography? Photography will continue to be a recording device, yet what it records is set free to be reengaged as a sample, bringing its various inflections to a new composition. The camera, scanner, or Xerox machine along with the pictures they produce can often be understood as parts in a much larger process, perhaps resulting in a final product that may not even be a photograph. Photography and photographic practices become technical applications with which to synthesize these various sources. Such approaches are in sync with the way our culture creates art from our increasingly fragmented experiences—by using technology to stitch together new forms of expression that evaluate, exploit, or question the systems and paradigms that have brought about our current condition.

Through the works they produce, artists who practice image transfer respond to the hectic way we experience and process visual information. Their sensitivity to this state of overload provides us with insights into how these experiences are structured and what they mean for us. In many ways, image transfer art forms an important outgrowth of the expanding definition of photography in the digital era that pushes the once more circumscribed medium to encompass an intriguing number of considerations of the image's agenda in an increasingly photographic universe. Vilém Flusser concluded that the debate ultimately focuses on issues of human freedom.[15] To break away from technology's control, we must understand its operations and use its apparatuses and products imaginatively, even humanistically. Artists experimenting with photographic practices and the dominant image culture attempt just that.

15 Flusser, 82.

SEAN DACK

KARL HAENDEL

JORDAN KANTOR

MATT KEEGAN

CARTER MULL

LISA OPPENHEIM

MARLO PASCUAL

AMANDA ROSS-HO

SARA VANDERBEEK

SIEBREN VERSTEEG

ERIKA VOGT

KELLEY WALKER

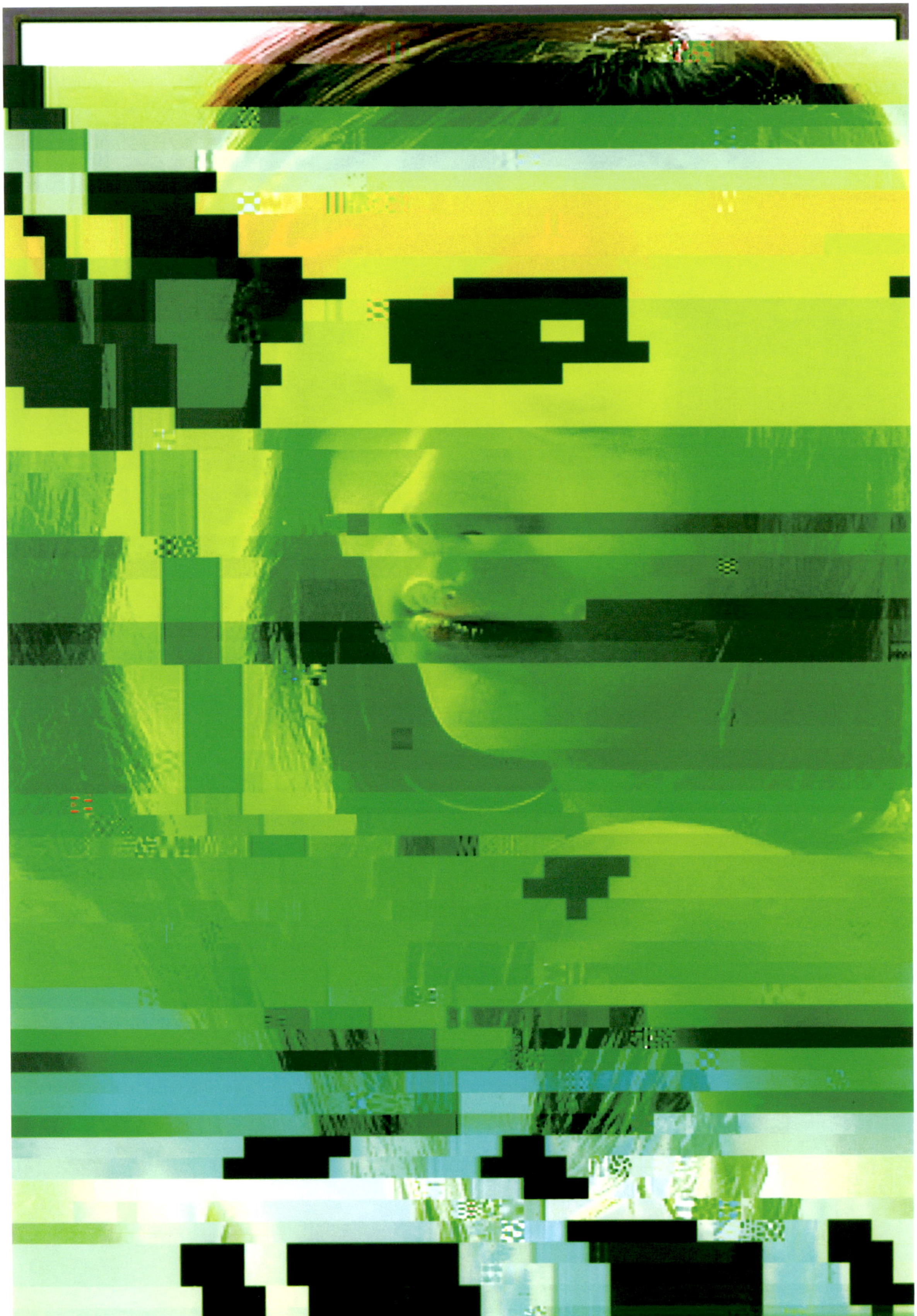

Sean Dack
Glitch Girl #4. 2008
Chromogenic print

SEAN DACK

Preferring the "alchemical side" of photography to the mechanical, Sean Dack attempts to conjure the "ghosts" within an image by exploiting misapplications and mistakes in processing to reveal a mysterious or unexpected image. For a current body of work, Dack manipulates images shot with his own camera and images found online; he makes no hierarchical value judgments about the use of either. He corrupts the digital file by skewing, moving, and accentuating pixels, and heightening or changing coloration. Dack sees digitization itself as a process of abstraction. He looks for moments in this translation or migration where a loss of information may occur. The resulting compositions mix depiction with design and simultaneously reveal and conceal their sources as computer code and pictorial representation. Each of his prints, though made from an infinitely reproducible digital file, is unique.

Dack's fascination with the infinite aspect of the Web grows from the nearly limitless capacity it allows for creative expression. Virtually anything can be downloaded and played with, uploaded and shared. Its magical ability to satisfy one's curiosity or desire in an instant guides his choices. (Wondering what a CIA rendition plane looks like? Google it.) His randomized selections range across a panorama of the early 21st century—from the architecture of our late capitalist age, to urban images from China, Dubai, and Los Angeles, and self-portraits people have posted online, among other things.

When several of these works are installed together, the artist arranges a sequence that meanders from image to image. Dack compares this to the corrupted, lost, and meandering data evident in the print. He also relates this visual map to "the way one searches for images or any other information on the Internet. It is a non-linear and inconsistent way of traveling through data and information. It breaks free of the traditional methods of hanging and installation and links us to a more virtual space we are becoming more and more used to."

Sean Dack
Clouds. 2007
Chromogenic print

Sean Dack
Building (Sir Norman Foster). 2008
Chromogenic print

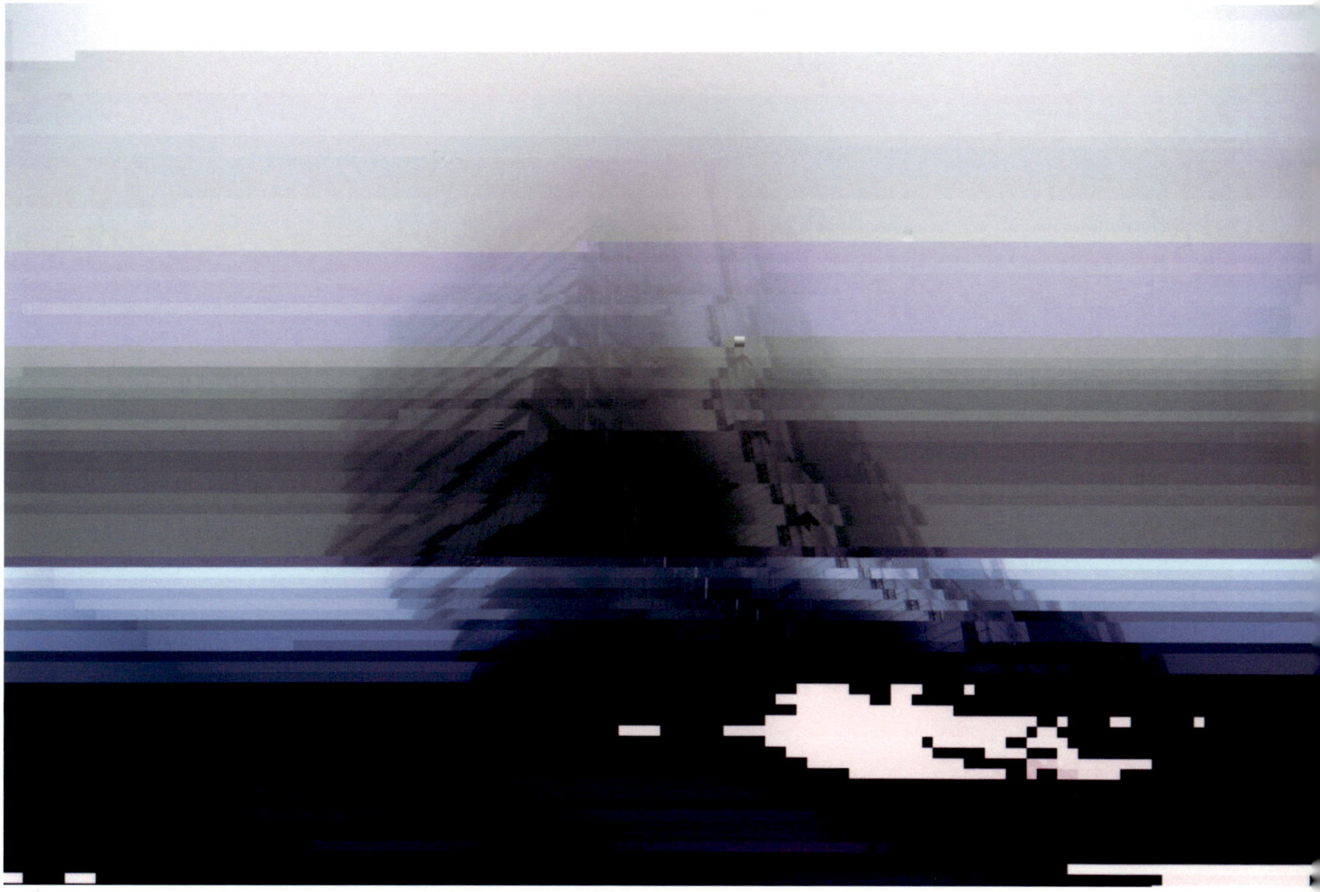

Sean Dack's recent photography invokes a new formal language created by digital interference. Since receiving an MFA from Columbia University in 2002, the New York-based artist has had many solo exhibitions including Ghost Hardware at Daniel Reich Gallery in New York and Echo/Repeat at Fredric Snitzer Gallery in Miami (both 2008). His work was included in group exhibitions at The Kitchen (2008) in New York and the internationally traveling exhibition Uncertain States of America curated by Daniel Birnbaum and Hans Ulrich Obrist. A 2010 fellow at Akademie Schloss Solitude, Dack has work in the collection of the Saatchi Gallery, London and prominent public collections including that of the Henry Art Gallery.

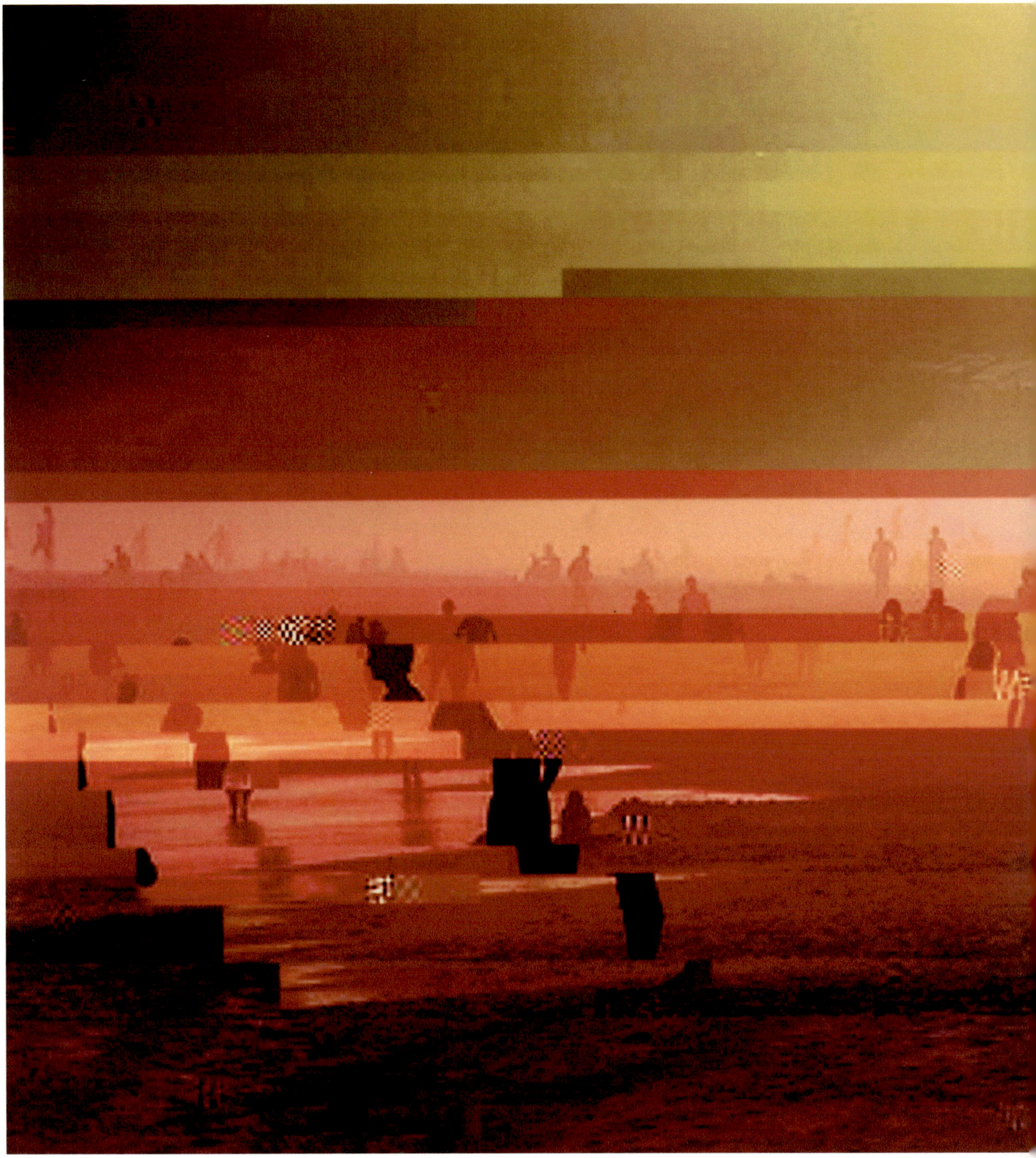

Sean Dack
Untitled (Beach). 2008
Chromogenic print

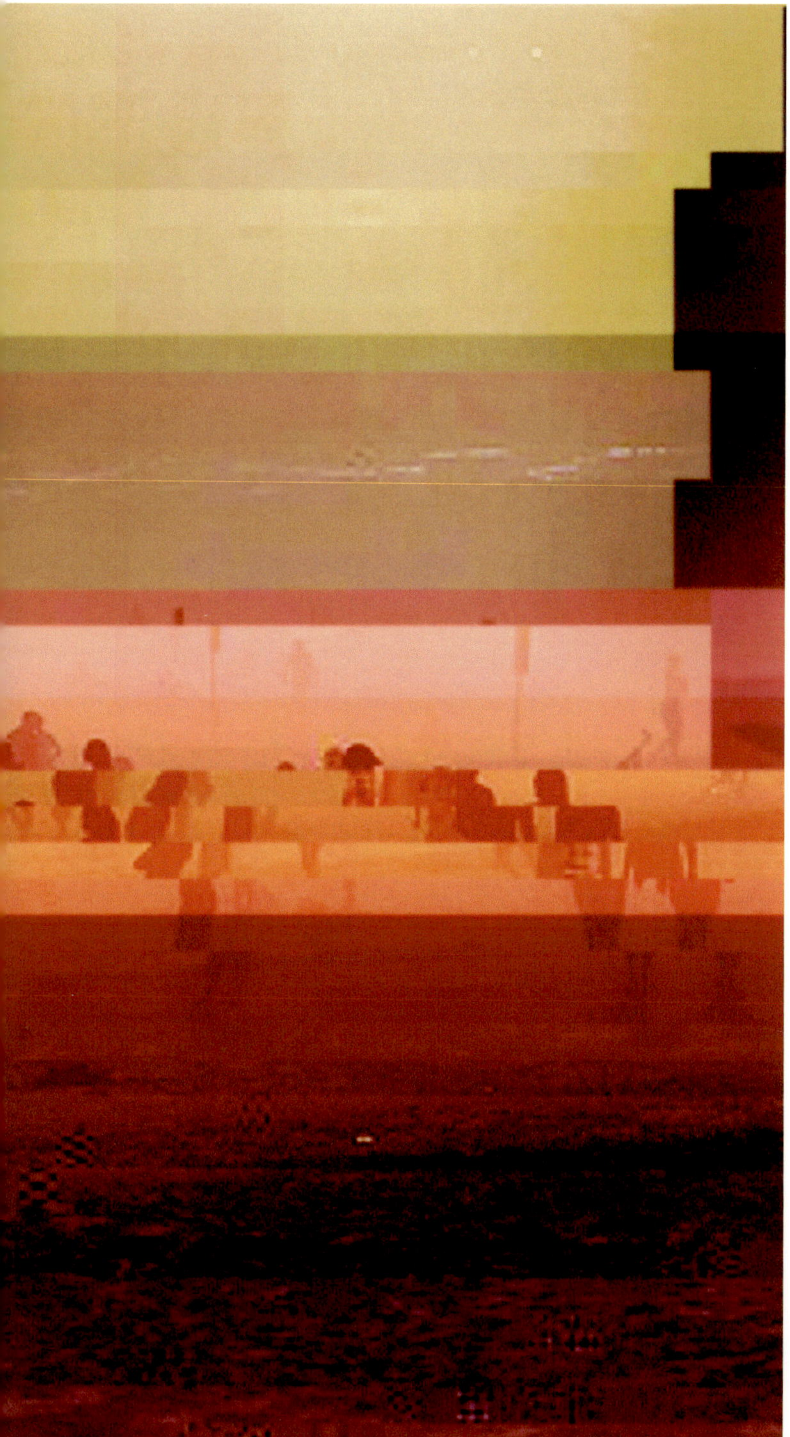

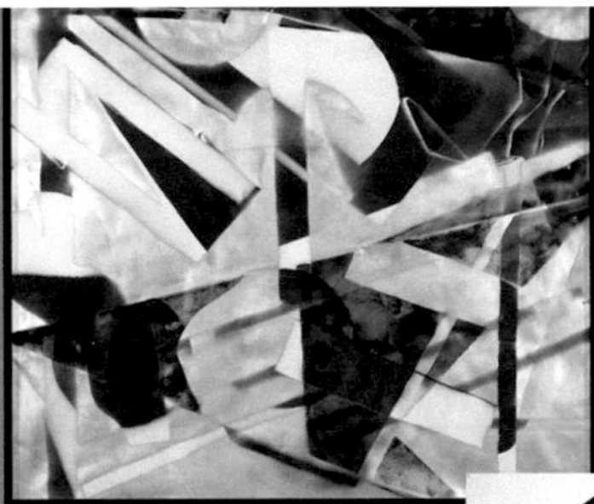

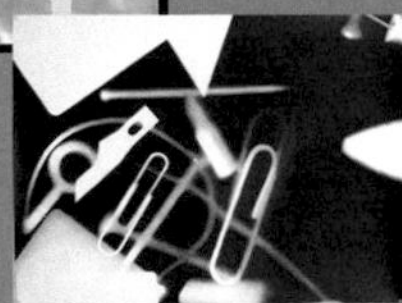

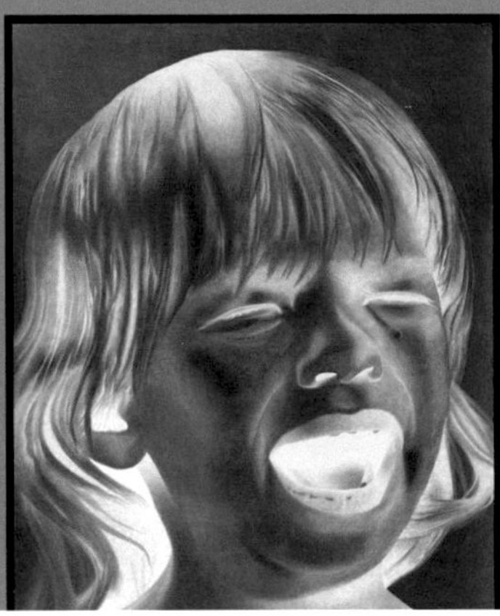

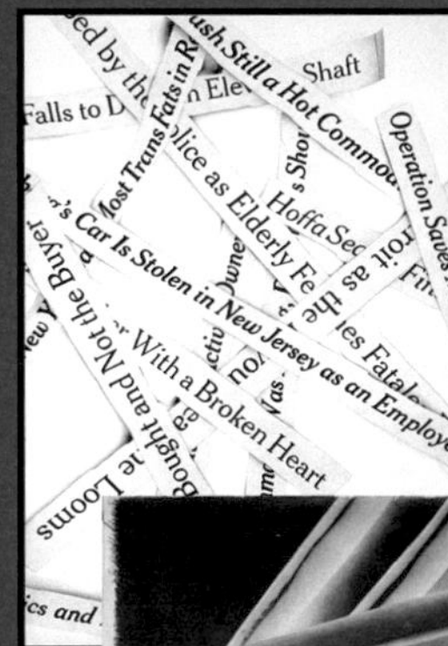
Falls to
Shaft
Still a Hot
Operation Saves
Hoffa
Elderly
Car Is Stolen in New Jersey as an
With a Broken Heart
Not the Buyer
Fatal
Looms

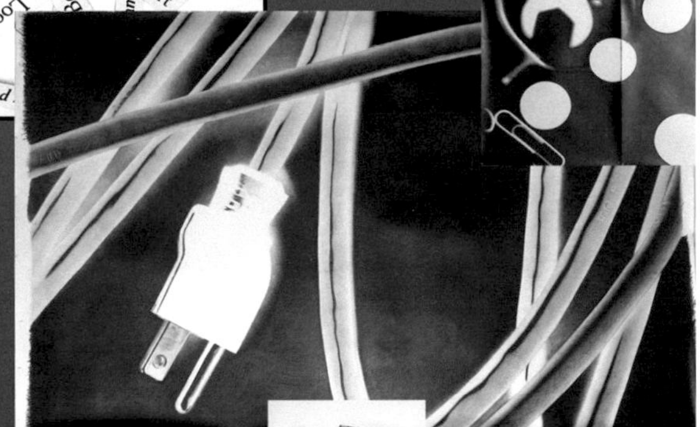

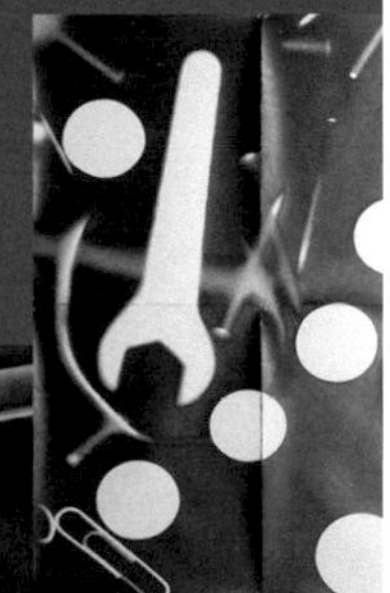

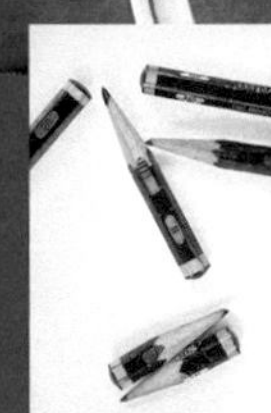

Karl Haendel
Image courtesy of the artist

KARL HAENDEL

To make his large-scale drawings, Karl Haendel often starts with a photograph that he has made or found, or a photo-reproduction created with a scanner. He projects this image onto a sheet of paper attached to the studio wall, and painstakingly reconstructs it with countless small pencil marks. Though it is an arduous process of manual labor, Haendel likens his method to that of a "straight photographer," someone with a camera who attempts to objectively record his or her surroundings and the events taking place there. He is quick to point out that the decisions made by a photographer along the way—from point and shoot, to crop and adjust, to save and print—ultimately yield a subjective view of what was first observed. He further complicates the drawing's relationship to the photographic source by emphasizing the humble materials of the handmade, blown up to a scale of size and of effort that verges on the oppressive.

Though his work may cause us to debate the value of original vs. copy, Haendel prefers not to situate his work on that familiar ground. Instead, he focuses on how a chain of iteration not only transforms a particular image but also allows for private readings and narratives to develop during the many steps of editing and copying. Because his choice of source materials always has a personal significance, he embraces how their idiosyncrasies inform a sense of self-awareness that arises

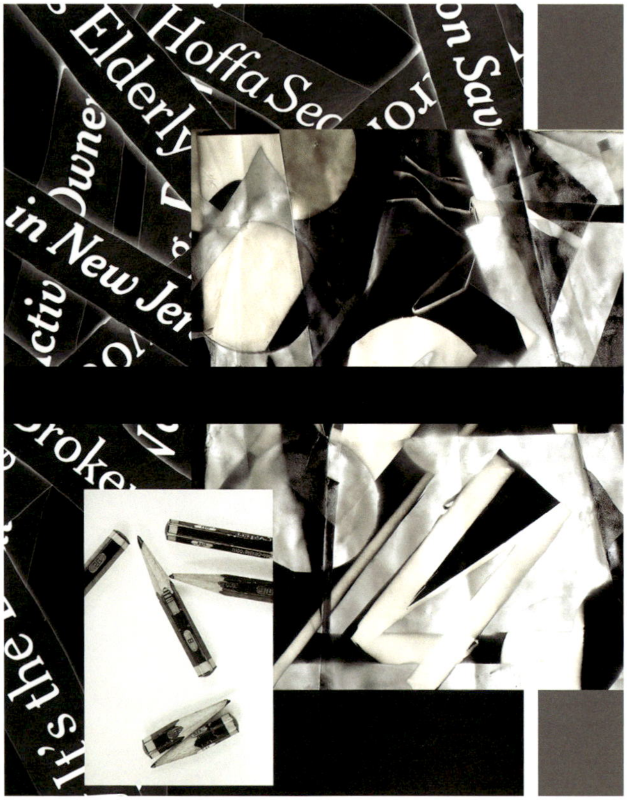

left and following pages:
Karl Haendel
Images courtesy of the artist

right and following page:
Karl Haendel at Lever House
New York, 2010

from the intense duration of the act of making a drawing. He cannot help but continuously reflect upon his choices and their meaning as he works.

In exhibitions, Haendel often crowds our field of vision by installing many drawings together like an outsized collage. Grouped, the drawings are relational and as such they form a challenge to signification; they suggest the potential for multiple meanings, dependent on context and arrangement. He also reanimates reproductions of drawings and past installation photographs as digital collages, as in the images published here. For him, each image is associative, not fixed, and available for reinscription regardless of its origin. The familiarity of these pictures grabs our attention, compelling us to try and decipher their story of the moment.

By combining personal and cultural imagery, Karl Haendel creates installations that comment on the American consumerist mindset and explore various means of image reproduction. Since receiving an MFA from UCLA in 2003, he has had solo exhibitions at Harris Lieberman Gallery (2009) and Lever House (2010) in New York, as well as Susanne Vielmetter Projects (2010) in Los Angeles and Milliken Gallery (2009) in Stockholm. In 2010, Haendel's work was included in Collection: MOCA's First Thirty Years (1980-Now) at the Museum of Contemporary Art, Los Angeles, and Haunted at the Guggenheim Museum, New York. His art is in the collection of the Whitney Museum of American Art, the Astrup Fearnly Collection in Oslo, Norway, the Guggenheim Museum, New York, and the Hammer Museum.

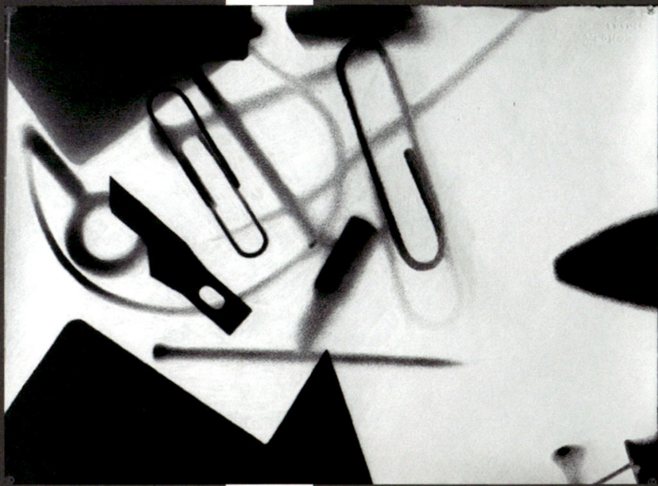

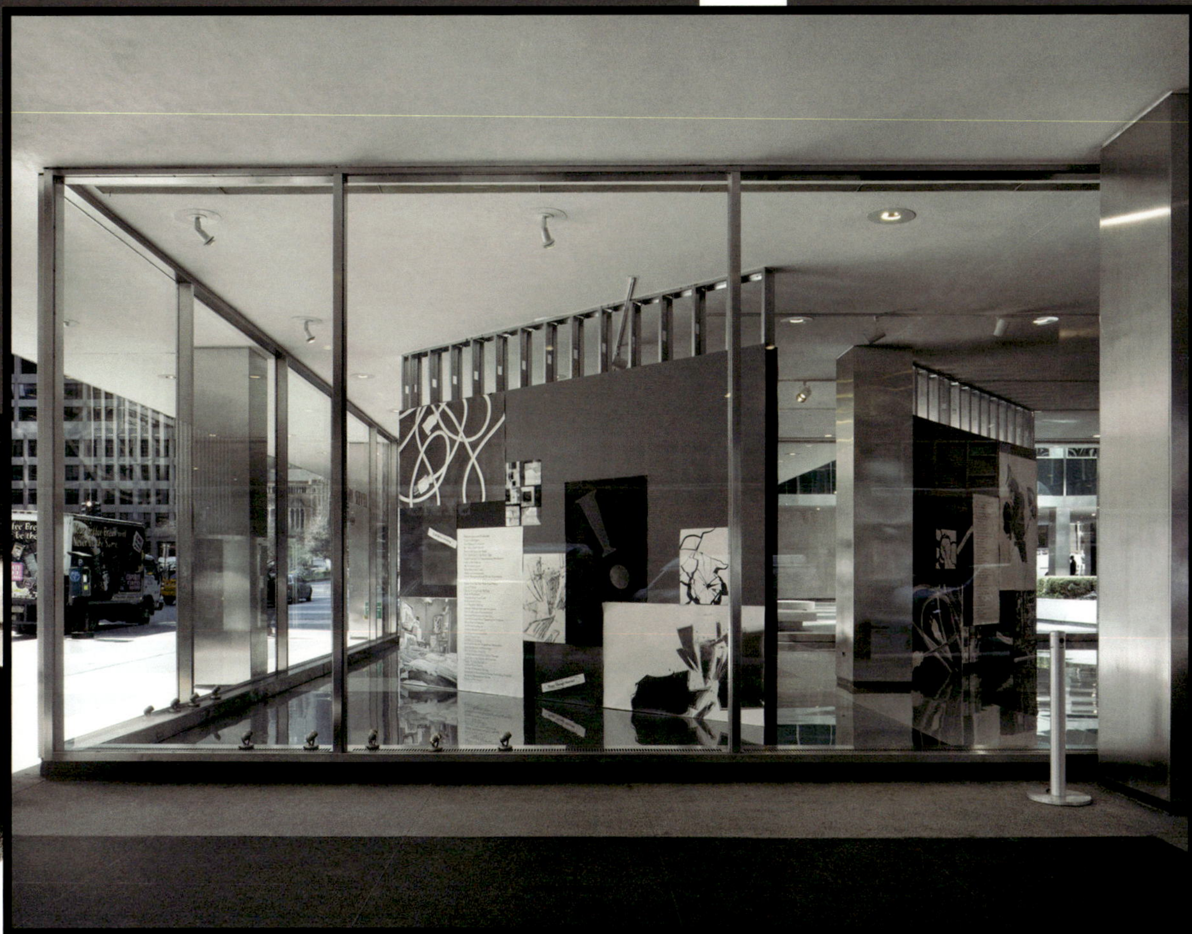

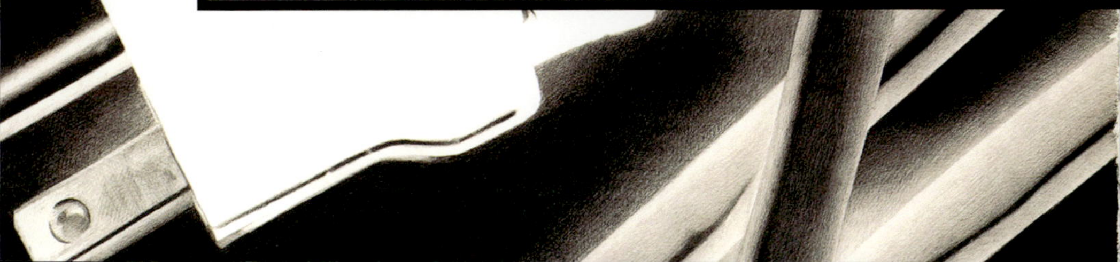

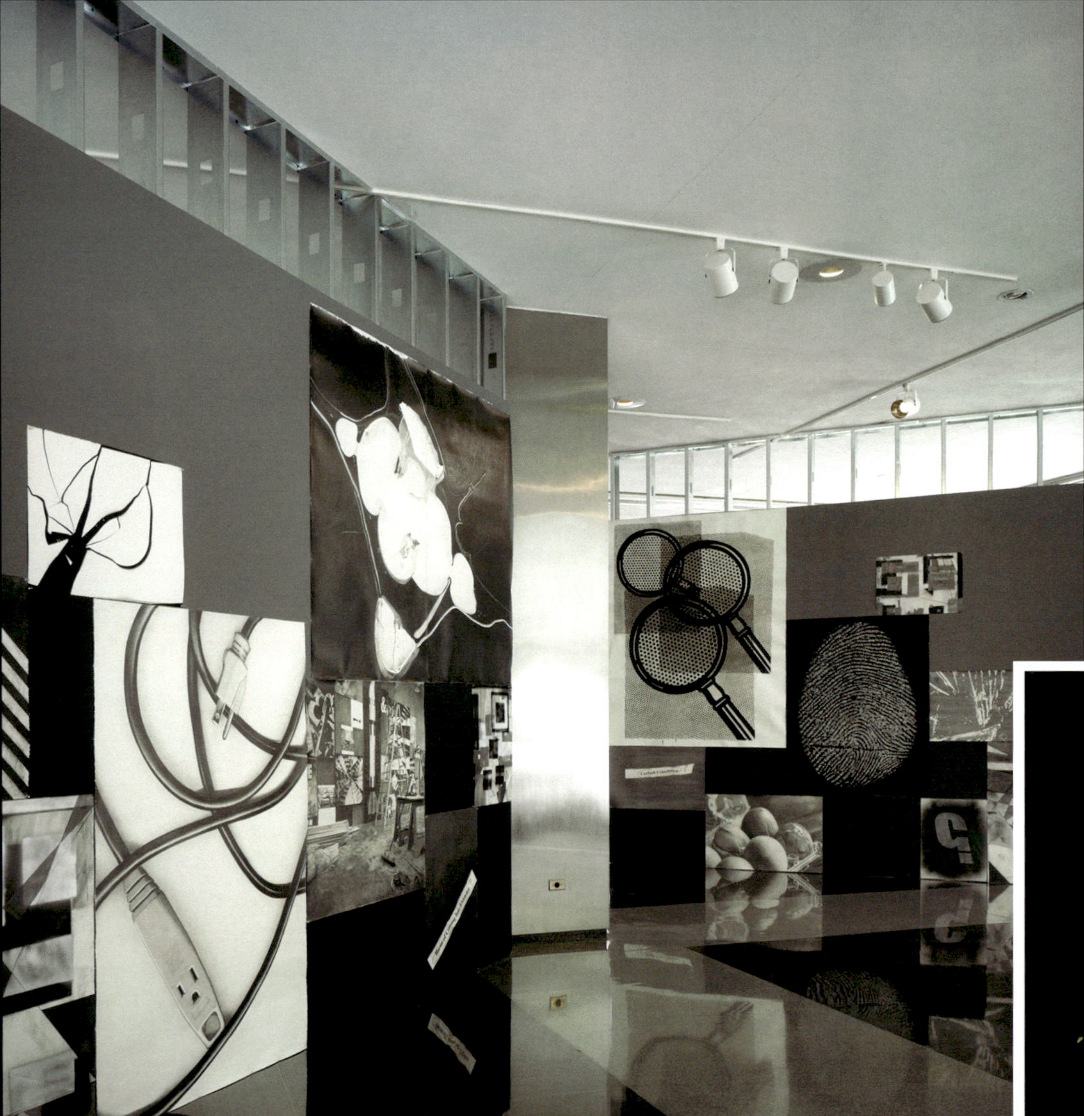

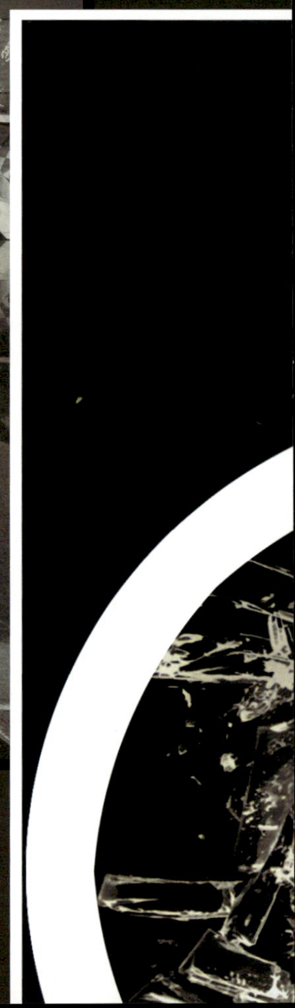

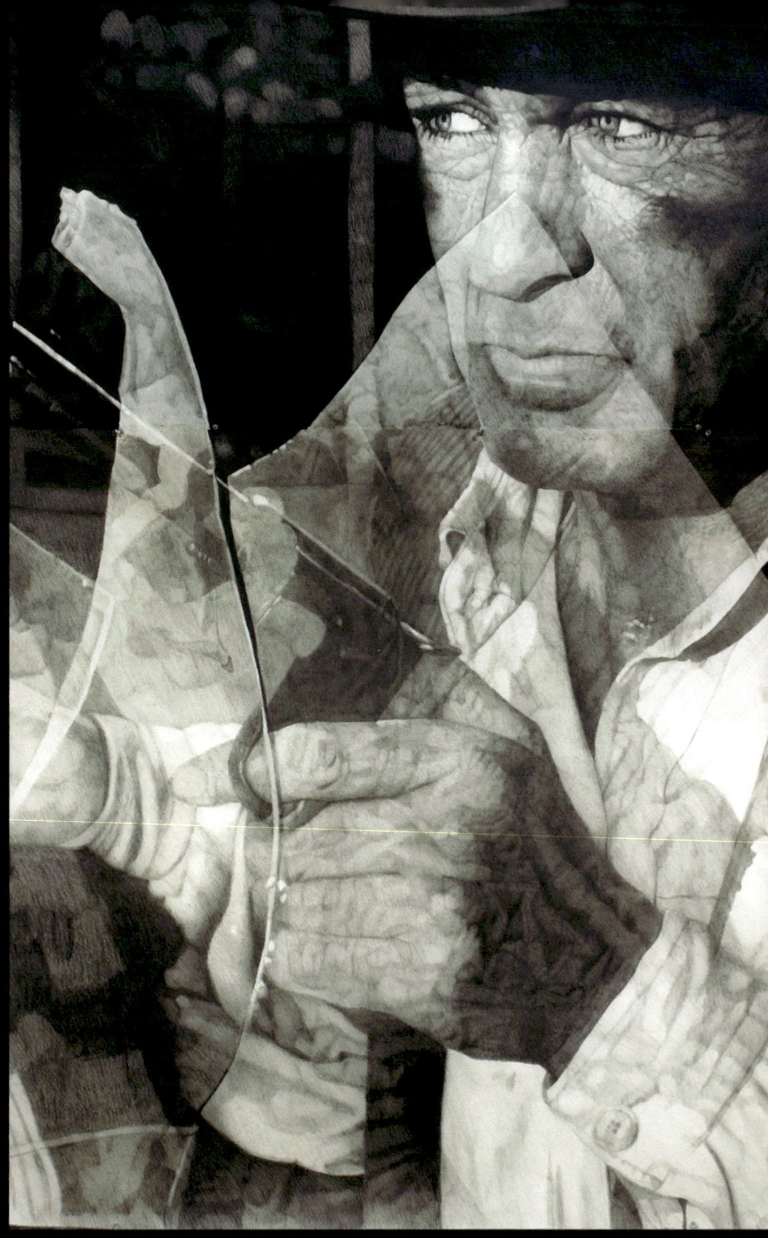

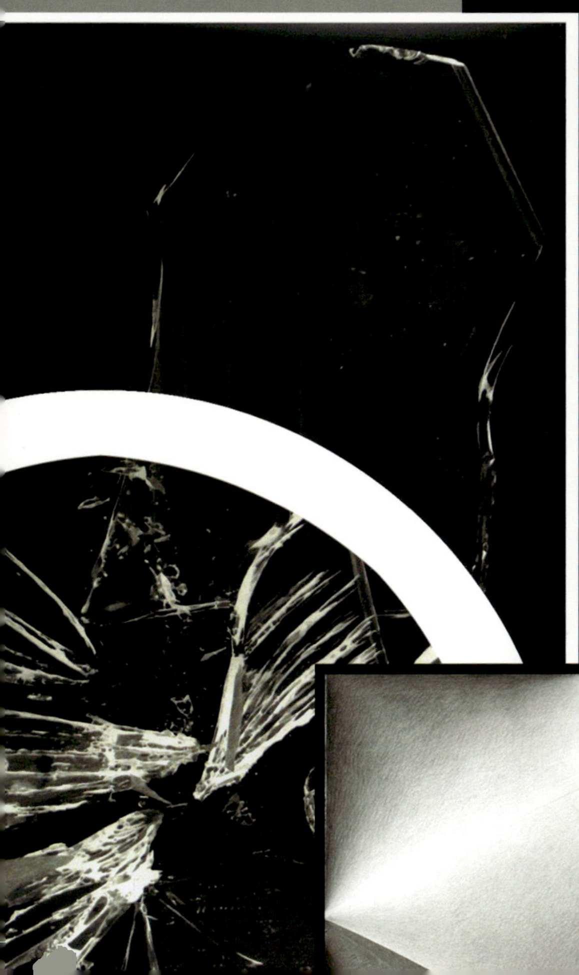

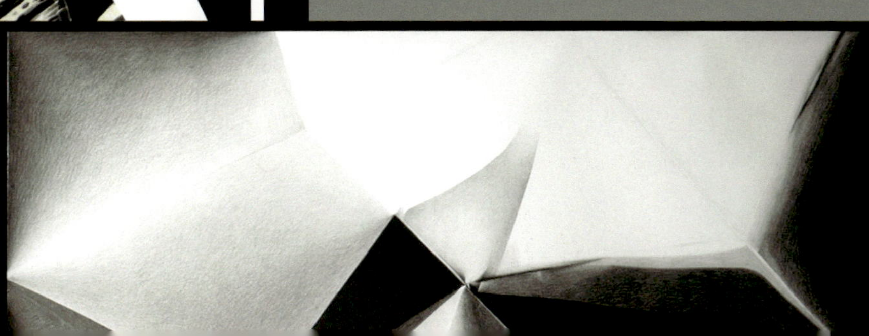

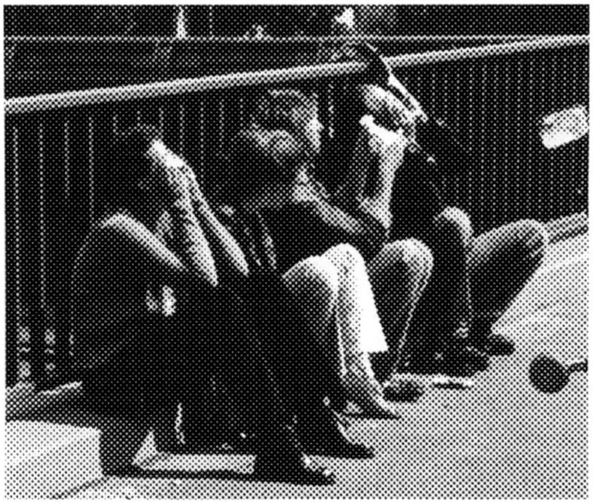

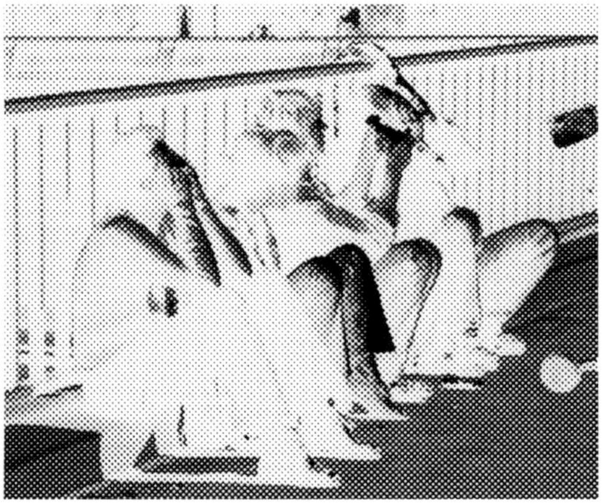

Jordan Kantor
Eclipse. 2009
Five screenprints on clear polycarbonate and silver Mylar sheets

JORDAN KANTOR

A painter, Jordan Kantor often begins with pictures from books, newspapers, and other printed matter. He then scans and digitally crops and compresses a source image before translating it into a painting. In part, he employs these tactics to isolate an image from its original context with the aim of opening up new readings of it and questioning the image's role as a record of information. Through the steps of the artist's process, an image also changes physically and perceptually as it moves from one format to the other, encouraging us to contemplate more critically what we see and how we see it.

Focusing on these moments of translation, Kantor has created a number of works based on a photograph that he took of people viewing a solar eclipse through a

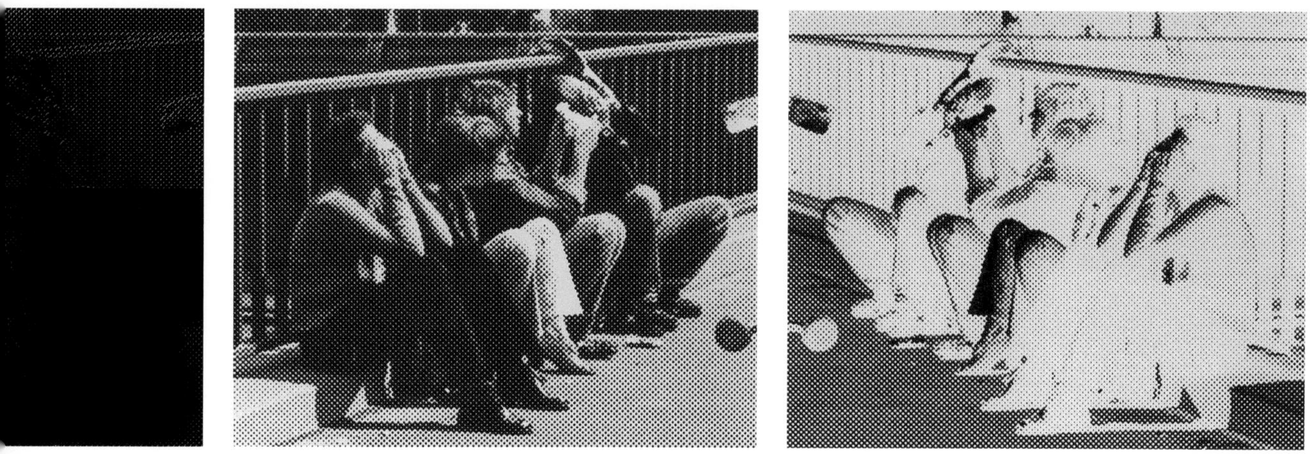

metallic film to protect their eyes. Viewing an eclipse is an apt metaphor for Kantor's methodology because the source is only seen indirectly through mediating devices. Initially the artist made a drawing of the snapshot using carbon transfer paper. Years later, Kantor used the image again as the basis for an ad. He subsequently employed a

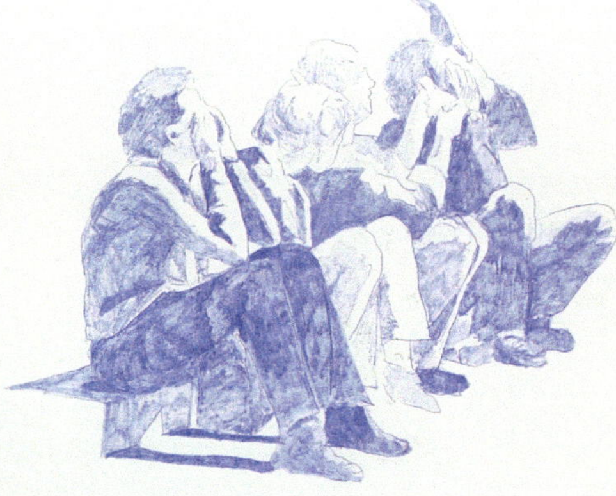

halftone and inverted image of it for a poster, and, finally, created a grisaille painting of it. A subsequent series of prints plays with different facets of photographic reproduction: positives/negatives and flips/flops, and even the belief in a photo as a mirror of reality. Other iterations—including a version in the separated colors of a photographic negative—continue Kantor's attraction to how an image transforms as it is reproduced in various media.

As an exploration of image circulation, the use and reuse of the original eclipse snapshot forms a kind of loop: sampling a single motif, and repeating it, adding slight variations each time. The sample—the casual photo—now exists simultaneously in the unique forms of drawing and painting; the reproducible format of prints; and finally ripples out through the widest channel of popular distribution as ephemera.

Through his paintings and prints, California-based artist Jordan Kantor investigates the impact of photo-reproduction, image circulation, and digital technologies on how we obtain information from images. A frequent contributor to Artforum, he received a Ph.D. from Harvard University in 2003 and is a faculty member at the California College of the Arts. Recent solo exhibitions of his work have been at Ratio 3 in San Francisco (2010) and Art/40/Basel in Switzerland (2009). Group exhibitions that have included Kantor's paintings are Kurt at the Seattle Art Museum (2010) and SECA Art Award Exhibition at the San Francisco Museum of Modern Art (2009). His work can be found in the collections of the University of Michigan Museum of Art, the San Francisco Museum of Modern Art, and the Harvard Art Museums.

Jordan Kantor
Untitled (eclipse). 2001
Transfer carbon on paper

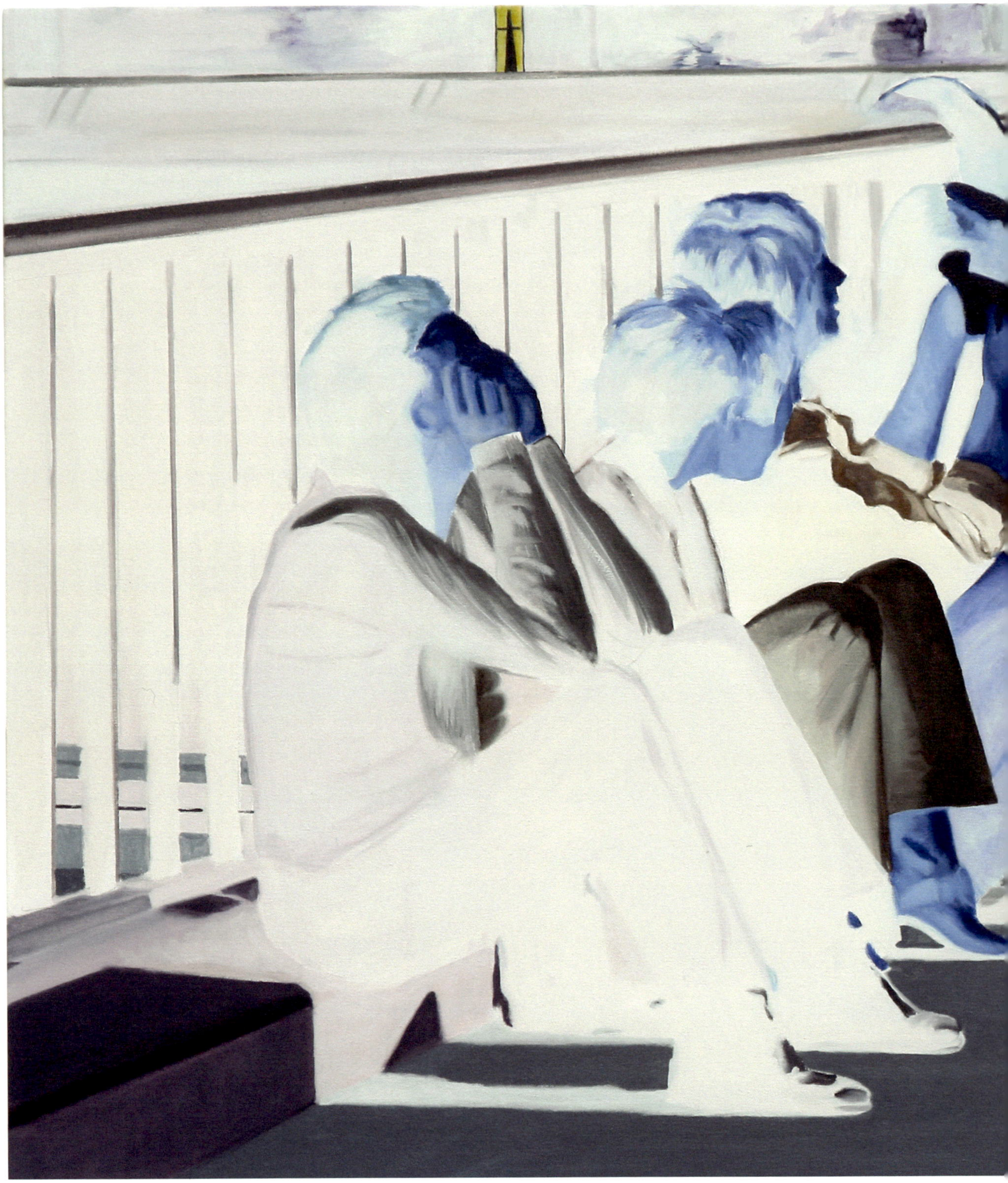

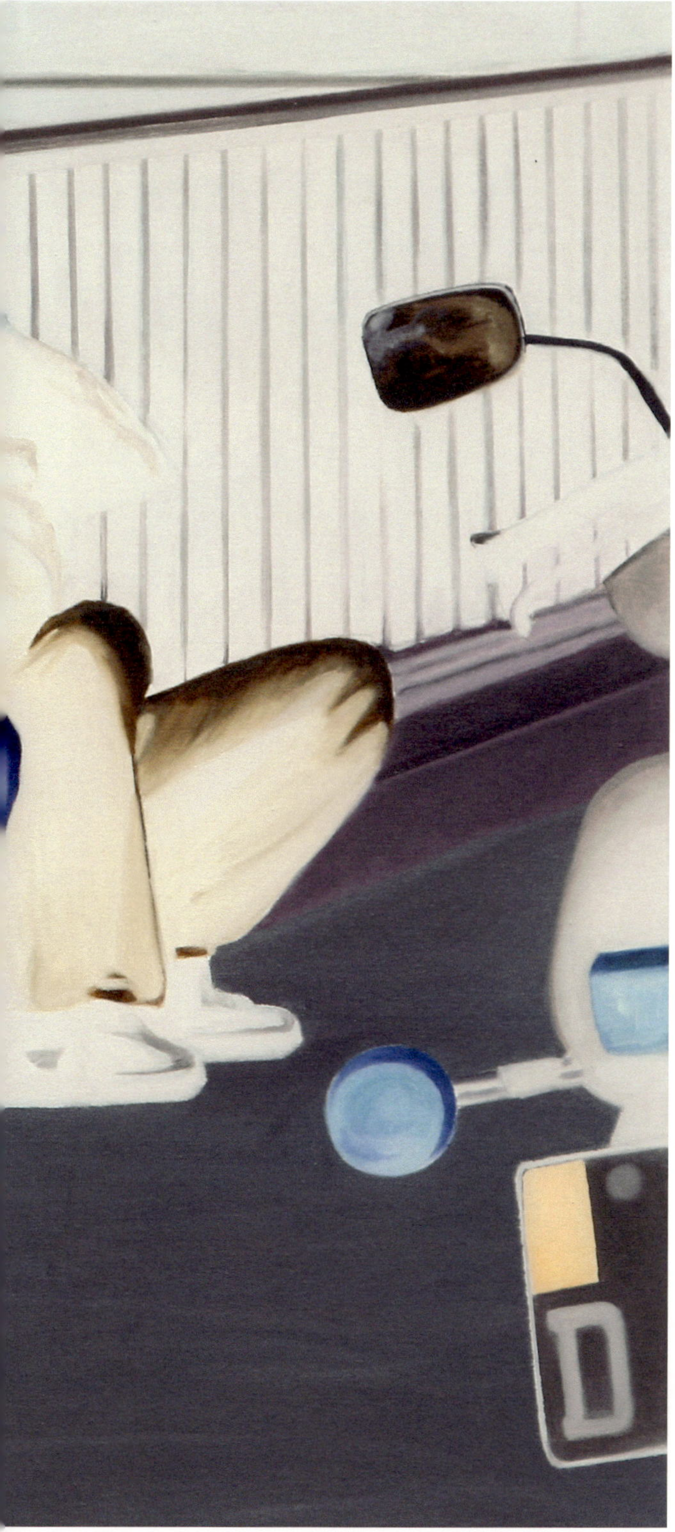

Jordan Kantor
Eclipse (color inversion). 2009
Oil on canvas

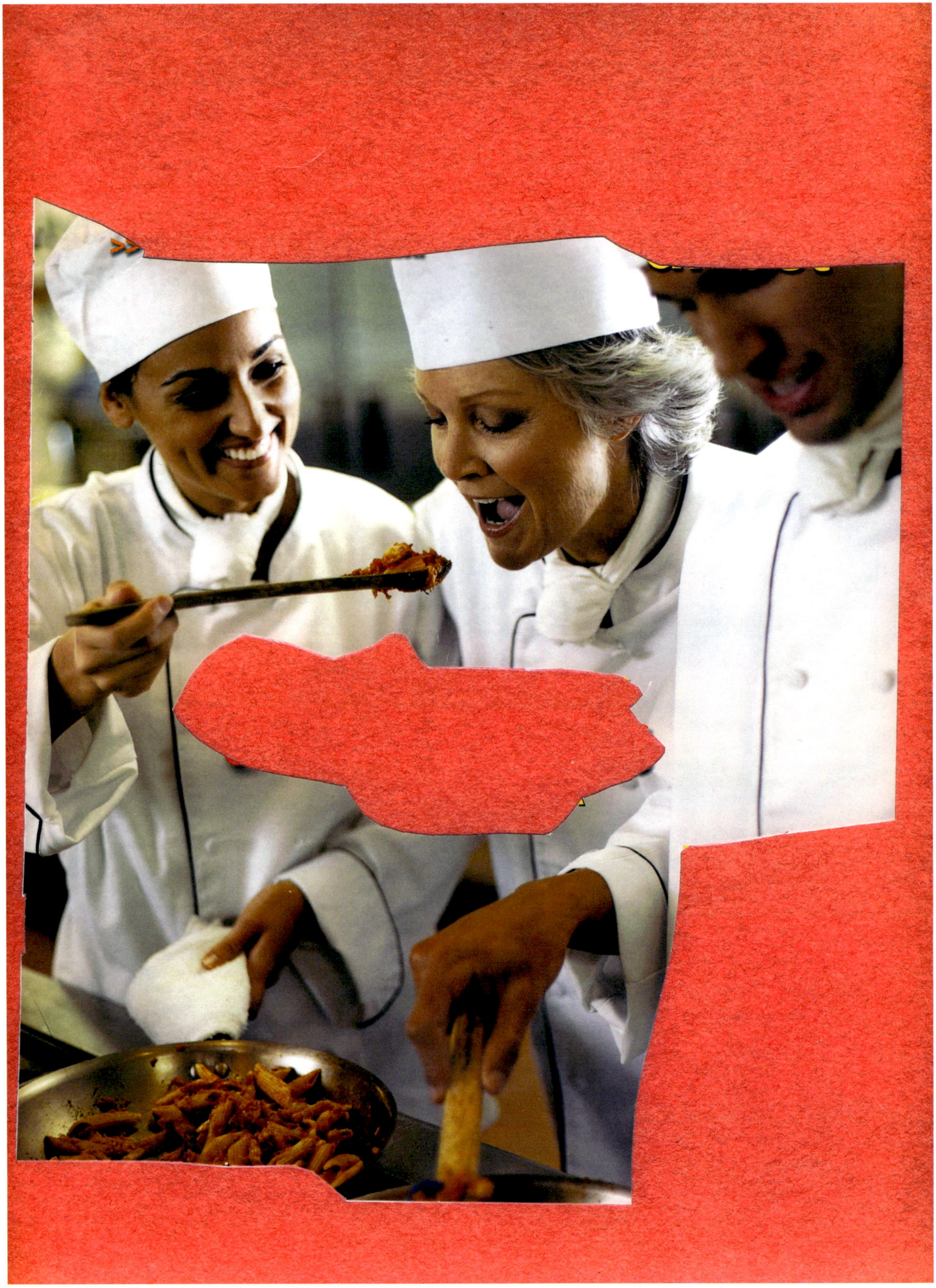

left and following pages:
Matt Keegan
Images are Words/Las Imágenes son Palabras (detail). 2010
Chromogenic prints, table with laminated images hand assembled by the artist's mother, two-channel video

MATT KEEGAN

Working with the photographic medium, Matt Keegan pushes against the traditional view that a photograph is a finite document. His work proposes ways in which a photographic image may surpass its usual status as a representation of a single event to function as a continuous recording of people, places, and moments across time. Whether accessing archival materials or using photographs of his own making, Keegan emphasizes the accumulation of meaning each image acquires as it moves through history and is seen in changing contexts. Keegan recently turned to the rich realm of stock photographs—those commercially available images widely used in advertising and other media—to explore the image's capacity to communicate without the mediation of verbal language.

Keegan's multi-part installation *Images are Words/Las Imágenes son Palabras* navigates this relationship. His source material comes from an archive of images his mother once used for English language lessons. During 20 years of working as an ESL (English as a Second Language) teacher for high school students and adults, she culled images from magazines, books, calendars, and newspapers. Originating as stock photos, these well-lit and staged images do not convey anything specific until they are placed within a context often activated by text. Because such an image's meaning can easily be shifted, depending on its accompanying promotional copy, pictures can readily be repurposed to correlate with specific words or phrases and become active pedagogical tools.

Through this project, Keegan attempts to negotiate broader implications of the making and viewing of such images. Stock photographs by nature exist entirely detached from an original context. To create them, photographers must construct images that fall into broad categories that are both malleable and anonymous enough to fit a range of situations, yet remain strongly evocative. As elements of visual language, they become the quintessential mobile sign. Dependent upon words and context to fix meaning even temporarily, stock photos will always remain unattached because of their availability for wide circulation and distribution. This condition upends notions of authorship. If the image circulates outside of the photographer's control, the situation may arise where no authority can designate what the image means and where it can appear. Whether this has a positive or negative impact on the creative and communicative functions of image-making is a matter for debate.

Matt Keegan resides in Brooklyn, NY. He works mainly with photography, collage, printmaking, and sculpture. Recently, Keegan has examined the myriad possibilities of archives, social history projects, cities, and ways to map and record time. He has had recent solo shows at Altman Siegel Gallery in San Francisco and D'Amelio Terras in New York and was included in Younger than Jesus *at The New Museum, New York (all 2009). His work is in several public collections including the Guggenheim Museum, New York, and the Whitney Museum of American Art. Keegan is also the co-founder and publisher of* North Drive Press.

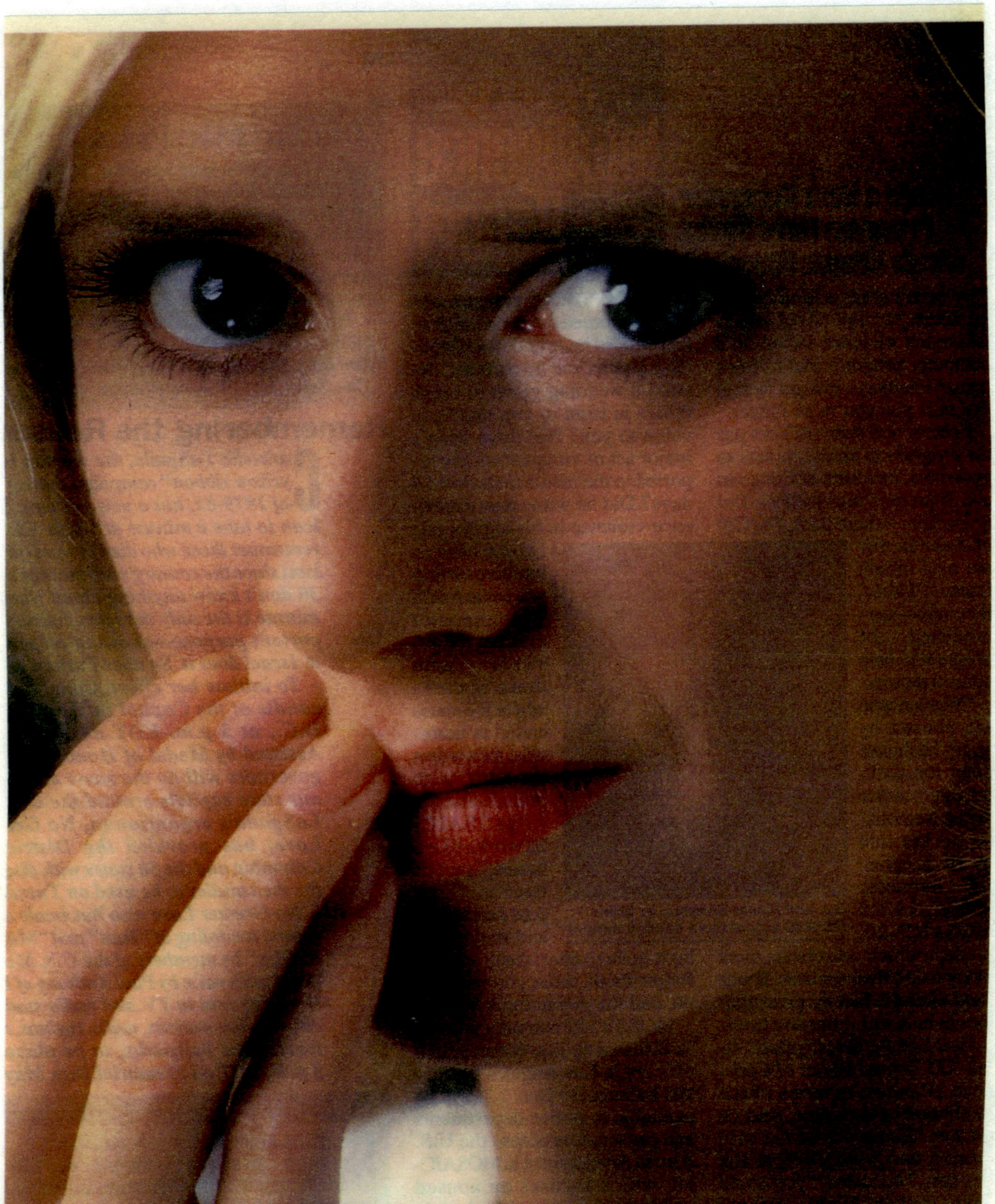

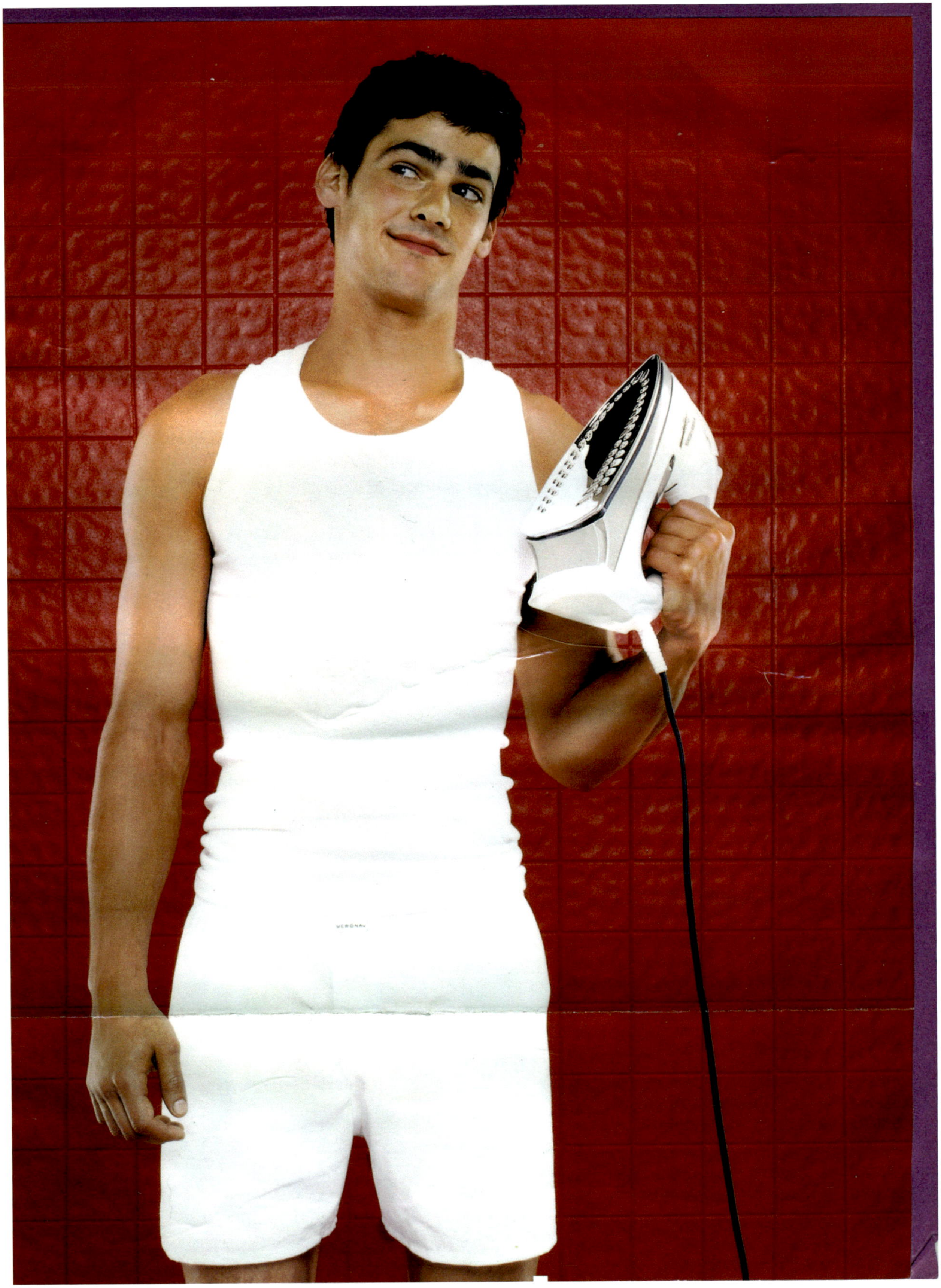
MERONA

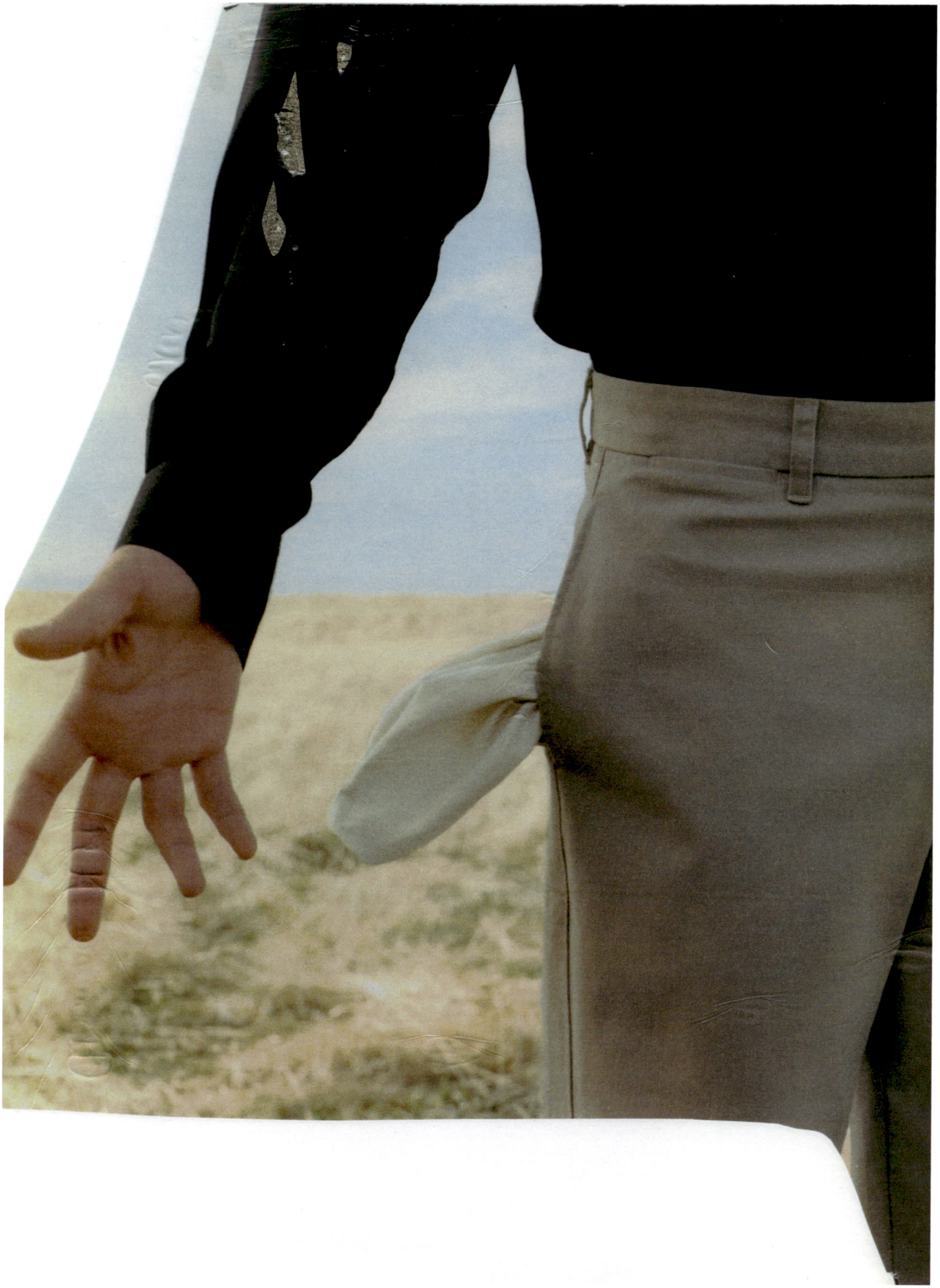

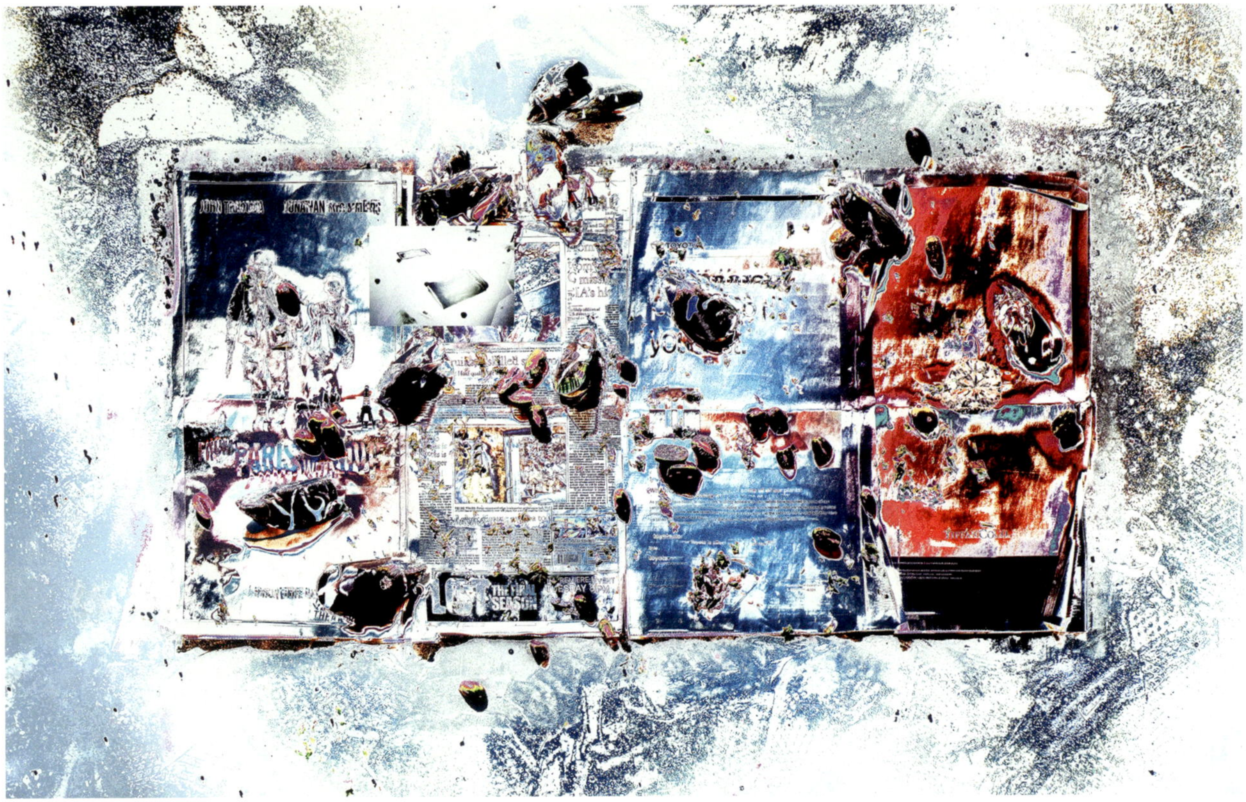
THE FINAL
SEASON

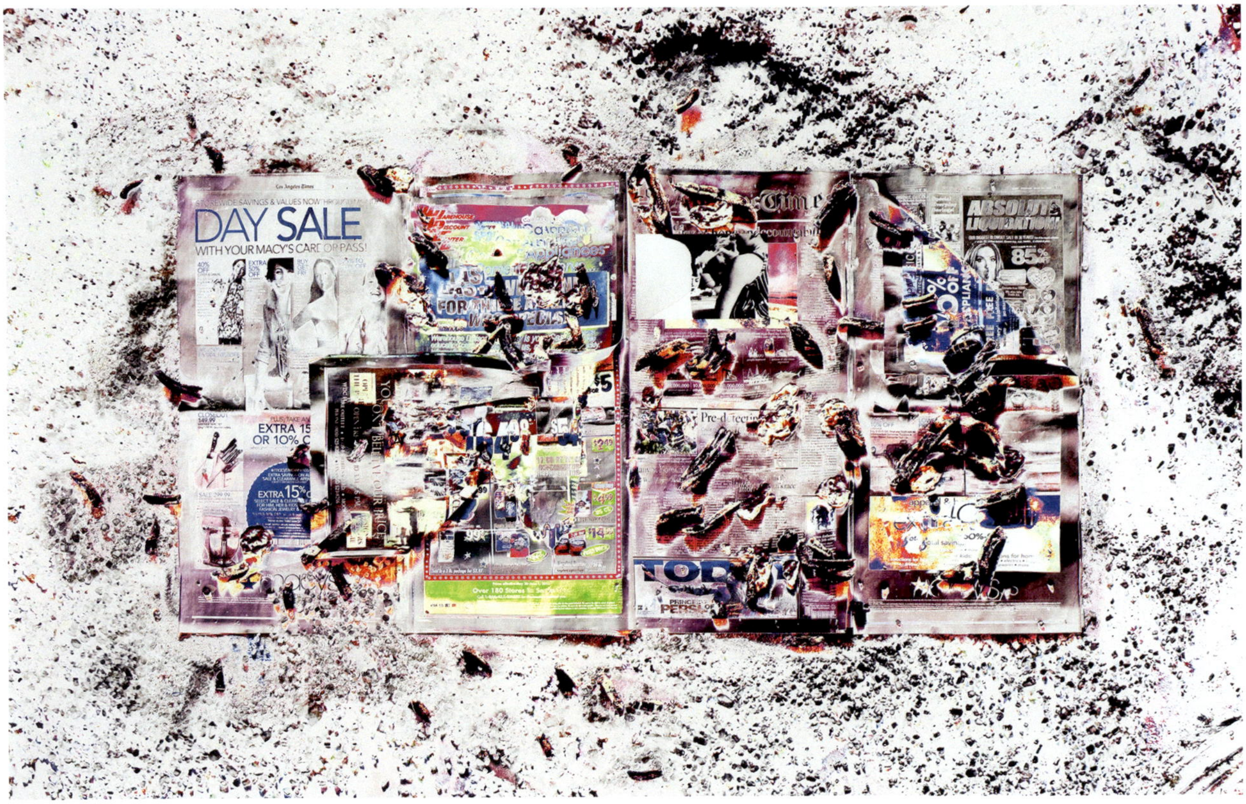
DAY SALE
WITH YOUR MACY'S CARD OR PASS!
EXTRA 15
OR 10% C
ABSOLUTE
LIQUIDATION

top to bottom:
Carter Mull
Expenditure. 2010
Type-C print with pasted print

Carter Mull
Passenger. 2010
Type-C print with pasted print

CARTER MULL

Carter Mull constructs his images in the studio, using extant photographic material such as newspaper pages, ads, wallpaper and design products, and photographs he has made. His layered photographs and drawings stem from his consideraton of the role that images play as personal and cultural artifacts. In a series of works, Mull utilized page spreads from *The New York Times* and the *Los Angeles Times*. Arranging pages so that back page ads carry weight equal to or greater than front page texts and images, Mull creates a blur of consumables: products and catastrophes merge together. The document is obscured in favor of a rush of visual stimulus.

Interested in the decline of print journalism, he turned to these sources to engage their ongoing role as markers of time and identity. For recent drawings, he explored "the consumption of information (as a consumer of *The New York Times*), time (as registered by the consistently generating archive and of the paper), and everyday life in all its complex relation to language and image." In this respect Mull considers his work in light of cognitive psychology, the study of mental processes such as memory, language, and visual processing. The many levels of information in Mull's work not only mirror our image- and media-saturated landscape but suggest how this crowded shifting field of vision infiltrates and transforms our perception of reality.

Mull aims to introduce a "different sense of temporality into image production." With regard to photography, his studio practice includes gathering and sorting source images, constructing tableaux, shooting a picture, and ultimately layering effects on the digital file using imaging software. Leaving traces of these procedures evident in a completed work of art goes against the grain of artistic, design, and commercial applications of technology that strive for seamless, though synthetic, images. Mull's application reflects his desire to treat digital files as material objects that bear the marks of his actions and processes.

Through re-photographing and altering existing imagery, Carter Mull investigates how we perceive language and meaning in photographs in today's image-saturated digital world. Based in Los Angeles, Mull received an MFA from the California Institute of Arts in 2006. His work was included in New Photography 2009, at the Museum of Modern Art, New York. In 2008, Marc Foxx Gallery in Los Angeles presented a solo exhibition of his photography entitled Triggers for Everyday Fiction. His work can be found in the public collections of the Hammer Museum and the Walker Art Center.

top to bottom:
Carter Mull
Horseradish, New York Times April 1, 2010. 2010
Ink on paper

Carter Mull
Over (April 7, 2010). 2010
Ink on paper

Carter Mull
Lobby, New York Times April 20, 2010. 2010
Ink on paper

following page:
Carter Mull
The Tar Pit. 2010
Type-C print with pasted print

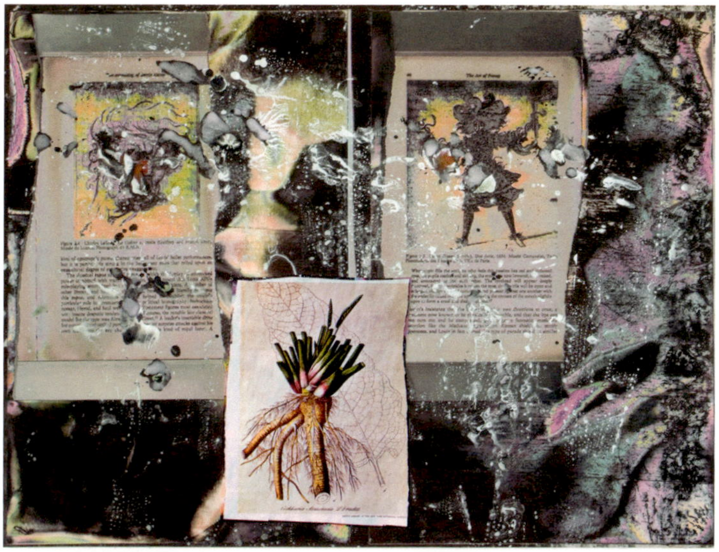

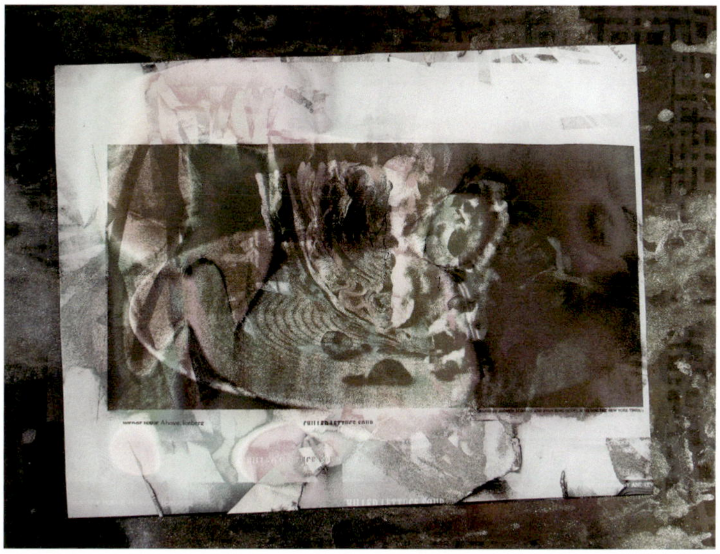

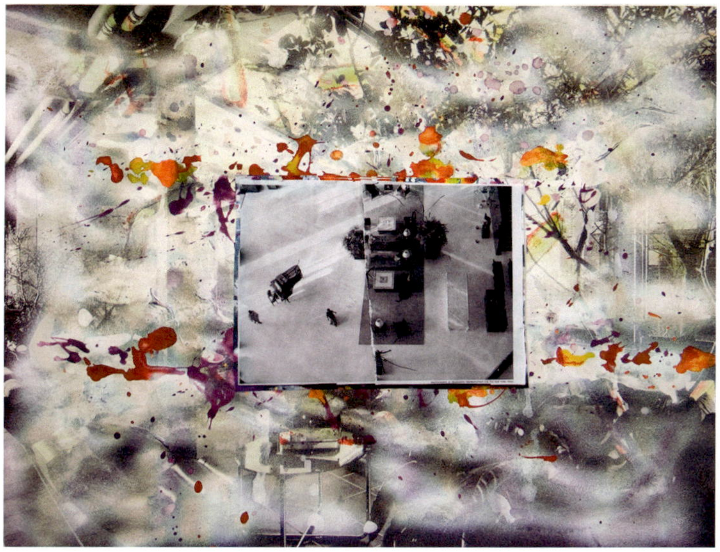

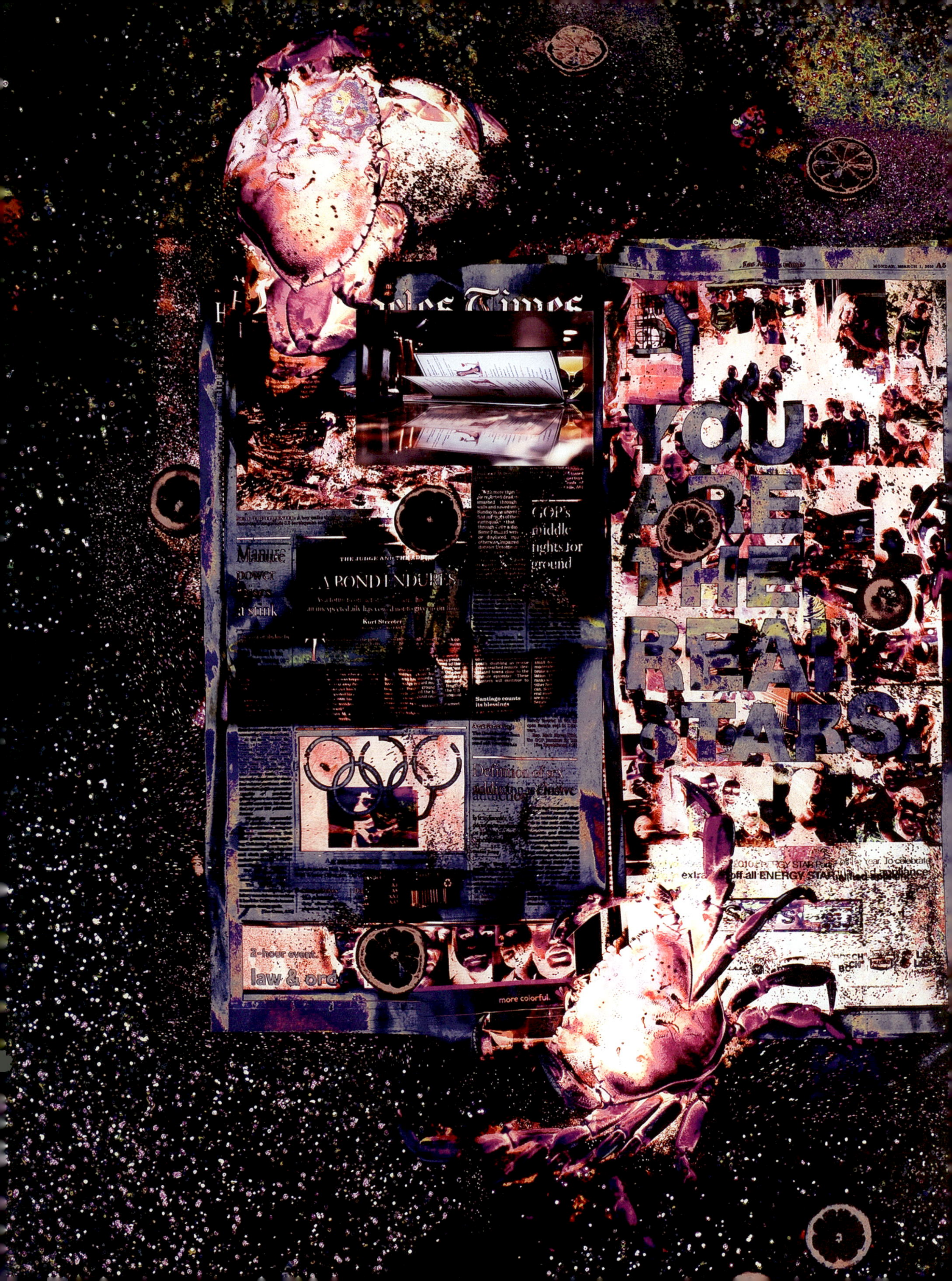

YOU ARE THE REAL STARS.
GOP's middle fights for ground
A BOND ENDURES
Kurt Streeter
Santiago counts its blessings
2-hour event
more colorful.

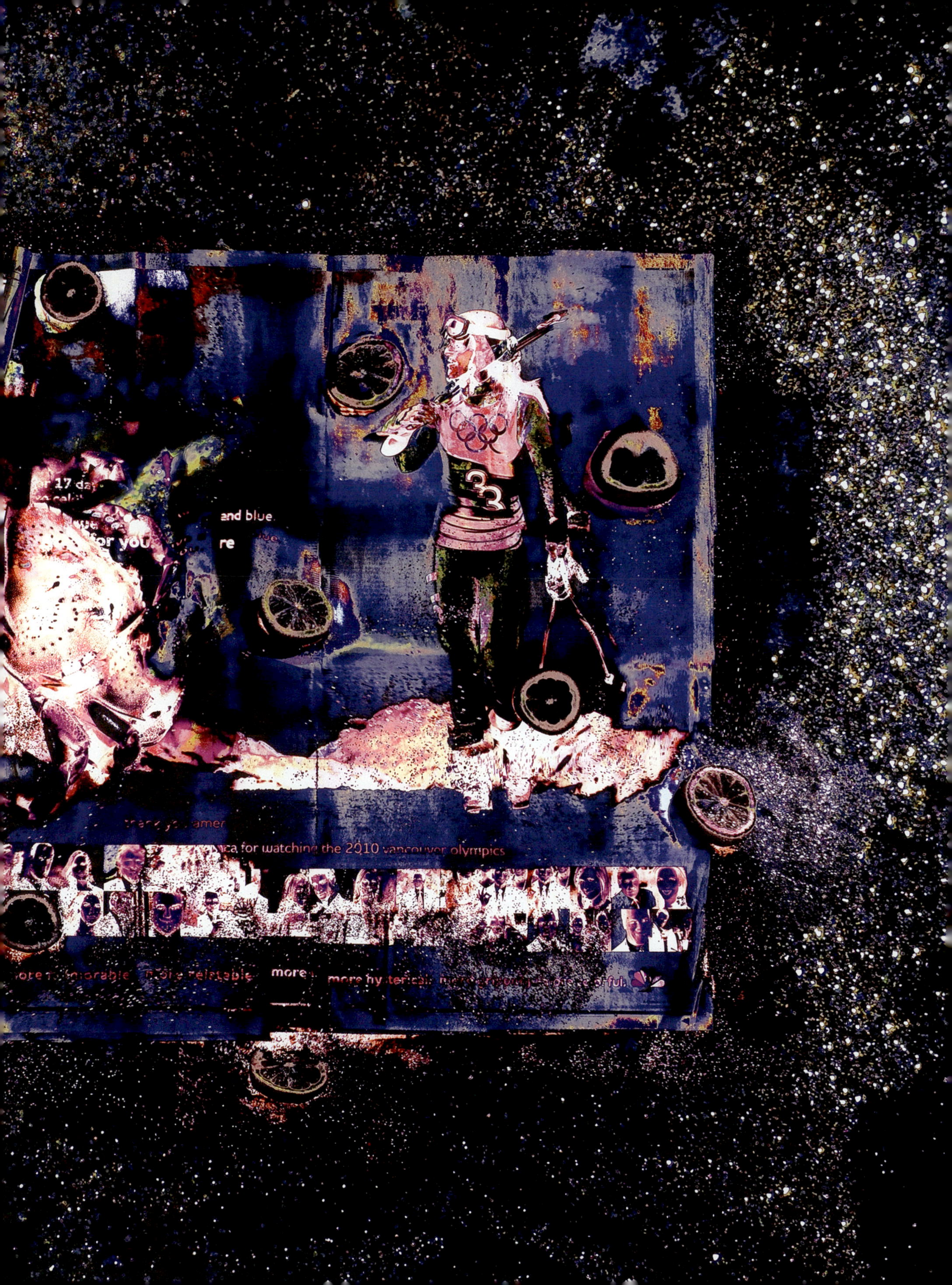
and blue.
for watching the 2010 vancouver olympics
more

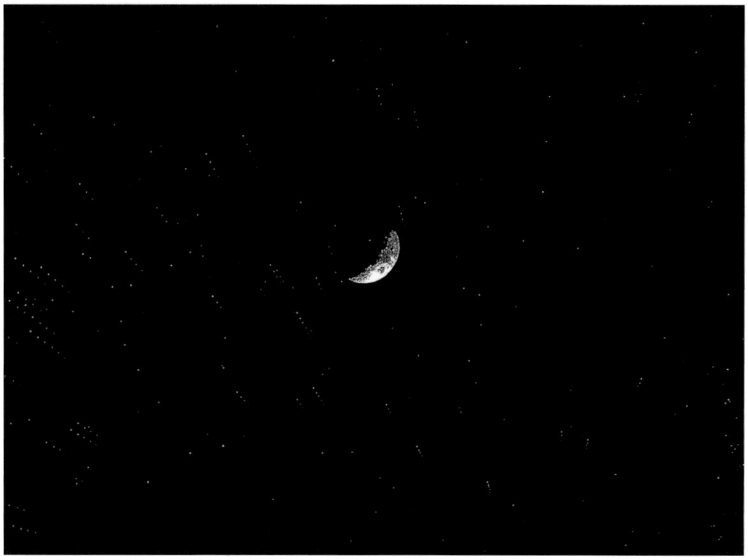

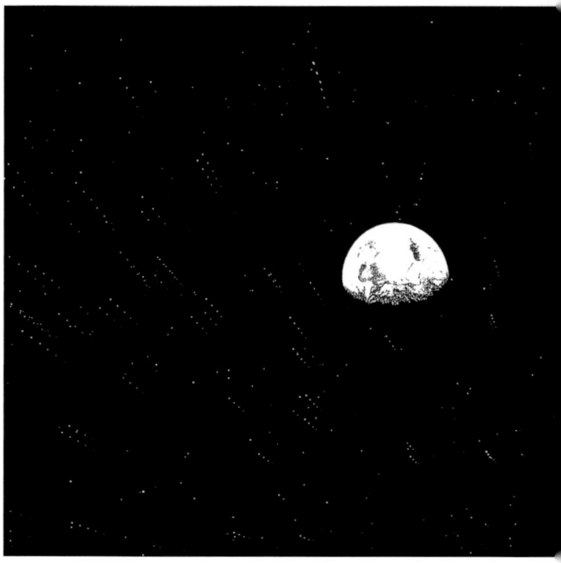

above:
Lisa Oppenheim
No Closer to the Source (July 20, 1969)
(still). 2008
Double 16mm film projection

right:
Lisa Oppenheim
No Closer to the Source (July 20, 1969)
(installation view). 2008
Double 16mm film projection

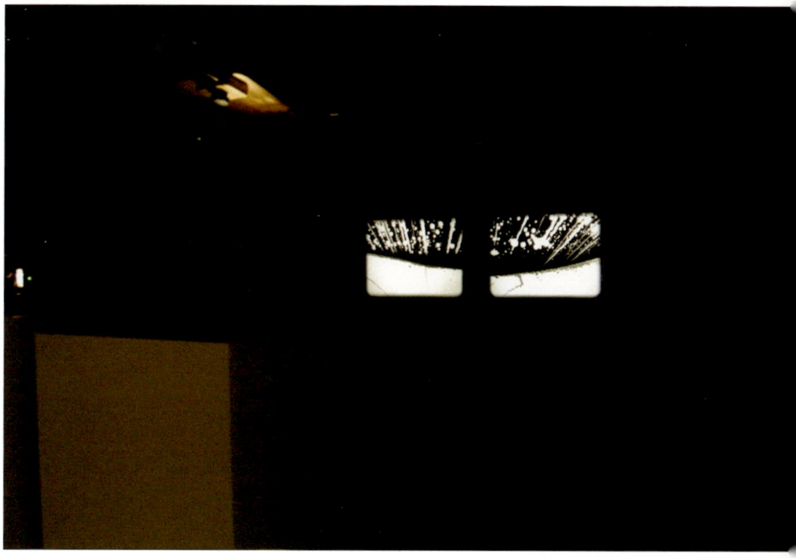

LISA OPPENHEIM

Accessing sources that range from Library of Congress archives to the photo-sharing website Flickr, Lisa Oppenheim seeks out representations of significant historical moments. Instead of iconic pictures, however, she looks for "remainders of the forgotten"—items related to the event but not central to its depiction. Her slide projection *The Sun is Always Setting Somewhere Else...* details snapshots of sunsets taken by U.S. soldiers in Iraq and posted online. The photographs do not immediately reveal anything of war; some are even Turner-esque, thanks to oil fires and dust storms. After selecting and printing 15 photos Oppenheim positioned herself in front of a sunset in New York. Stretching out her arm while holding each snapshot (a gesture previously made by photographer Kenneth Josephson), she then made another photograph, matching up the horizon line and inserting someone else's view into her own. The dual image collapses time and space, erases distinctions between locations, and suggests a cyclical loop of time, as if to remind us of the web-like interconnections endemic to our contemporary experience.

From her politically engaged perspective, Oppenheim also considers how the significance of visual information can be depleted or distorted over time as images are reproduced, disseminated, adapted to fit various agendas, and then eventually stored away. For a recent 16mm film project, she focused on the physical

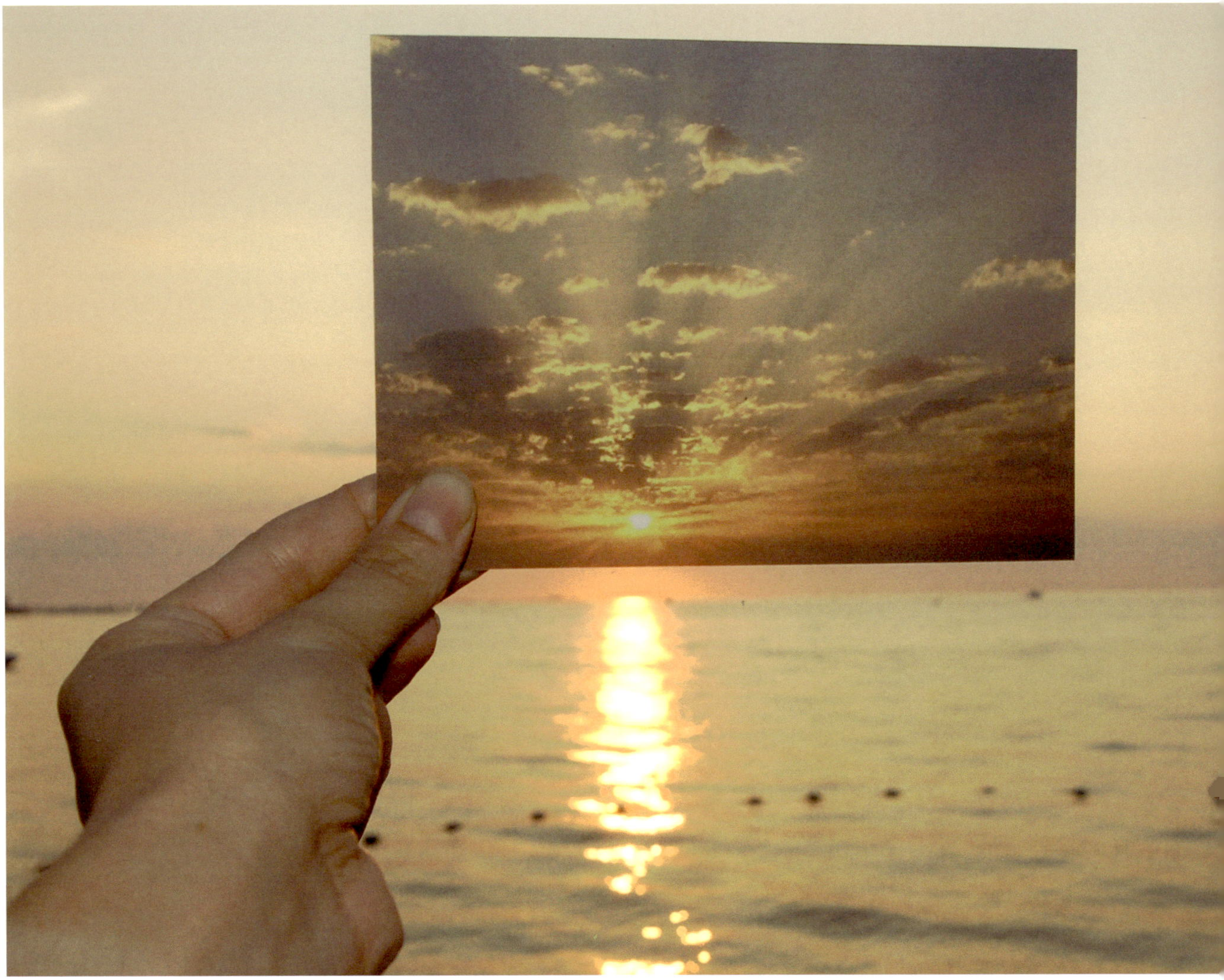

Lisa Oppenheim
The Sun is Always Setting Somewhere Else...
(detail). 2006
35mm slide projection, 15 slides

degradation of the source material as an embodiment of this process. The double projection *No Closer to the Source (July 20, 1969)* depicts Xeroxes of two photographic reproductions: one of the Earth and one of the Moon taken on the date of the first manned moon landing. Oppenheim photocopied these images at 101%. She subsequently copied the copy at 101%, the copy of the copy at 101%, and so on. Animating the many photocopies, Oppenheim presents the continuous distortion as a poetic metaphor. While the zoom (as a function of the copy machine, as well as the camera) creates the illusion of approaching each surface, it also suggests the starry skies of space. The physical reality of dust on the photocopier's glass transforms the copied image into ethereal celestial bodies. The title, too, prompts us to think critically about photography's reliability as an objective witness.

Through the reconstruction and appropriation of imagery, Lisa Oppenheim addresses historical and contemporary methods of producing, disseminating, and interpreting information. Oppenheim participated in the Whitney Independent Study Program (2003) and earned an MFA from Bard College in 2001. Her first solo museum exhibition took place at the California Museum of Photography, University of California, Riverside (2009). She has screened and exhibited her work at The New Museum, New York, tank.tv (London), Harris Lieberman Gallery in New York, STORE in London, and Galerie Juliette Jongma, Amsterdam. Living and working in New York City, Oppenheim is also a recipient of the Rema Hort Mann Visual Arts Award (2008) for emerging artists.

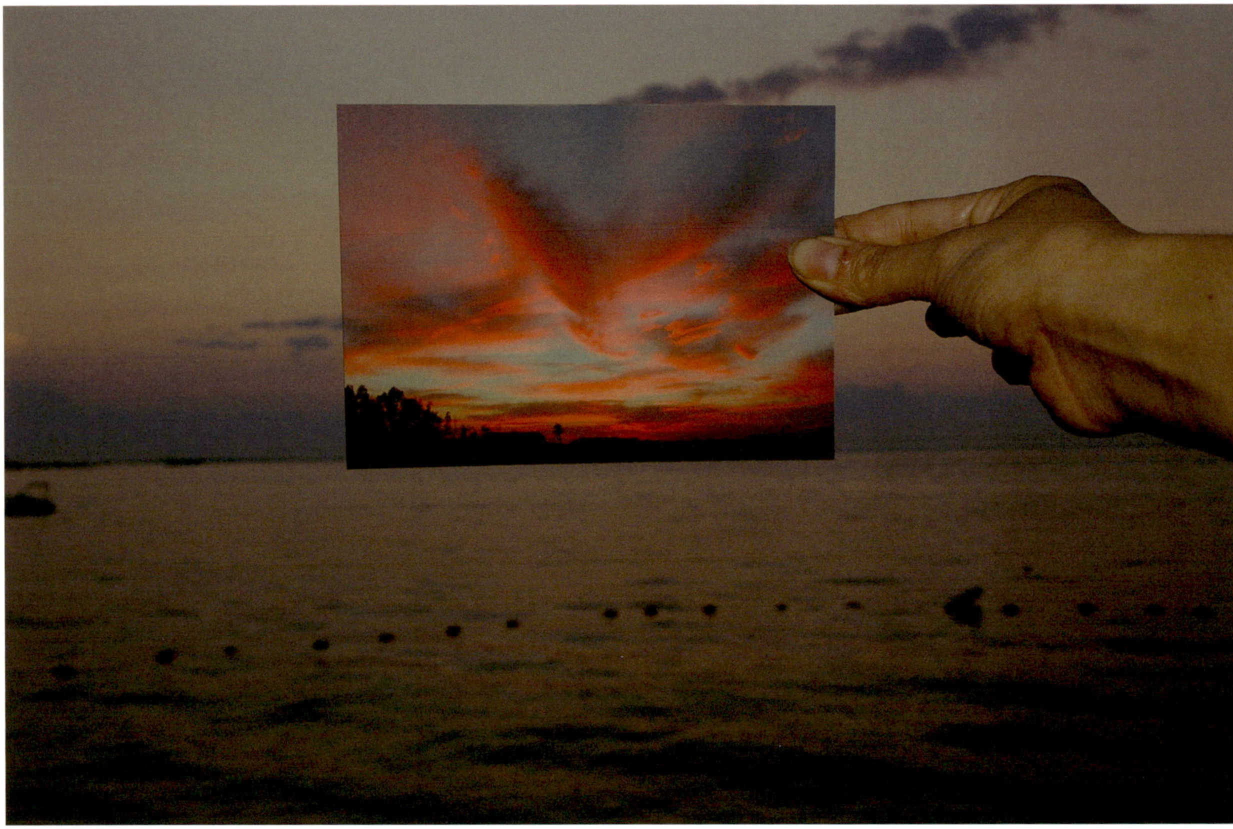

left to right:

Lisa Oppenheim
The Sun is Always Setting Somewhere Else...
(detail). 2006
35mm slide projection, 15 slides

Lisa Oppenheim
The Sun is Always Setting Somewhere Else...
(detail). 2006
35mm slide projection, 15 slides

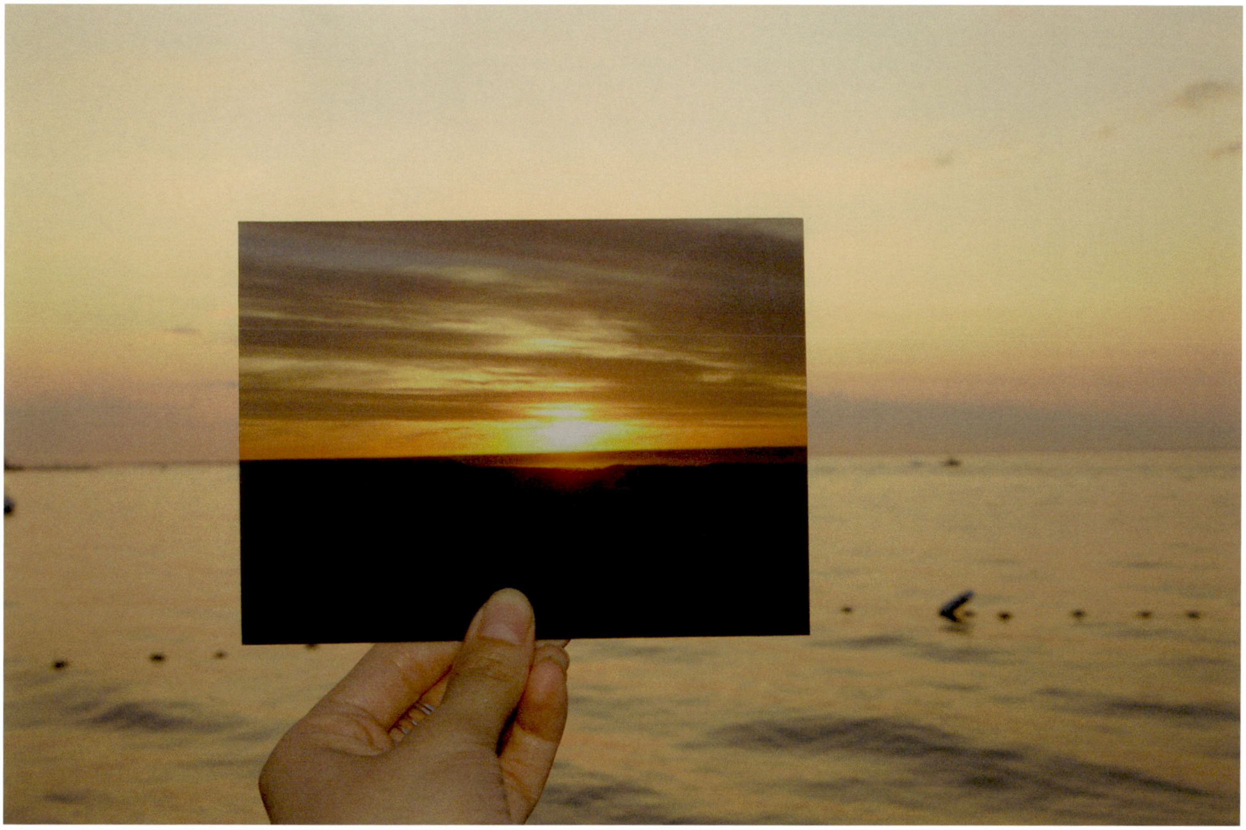

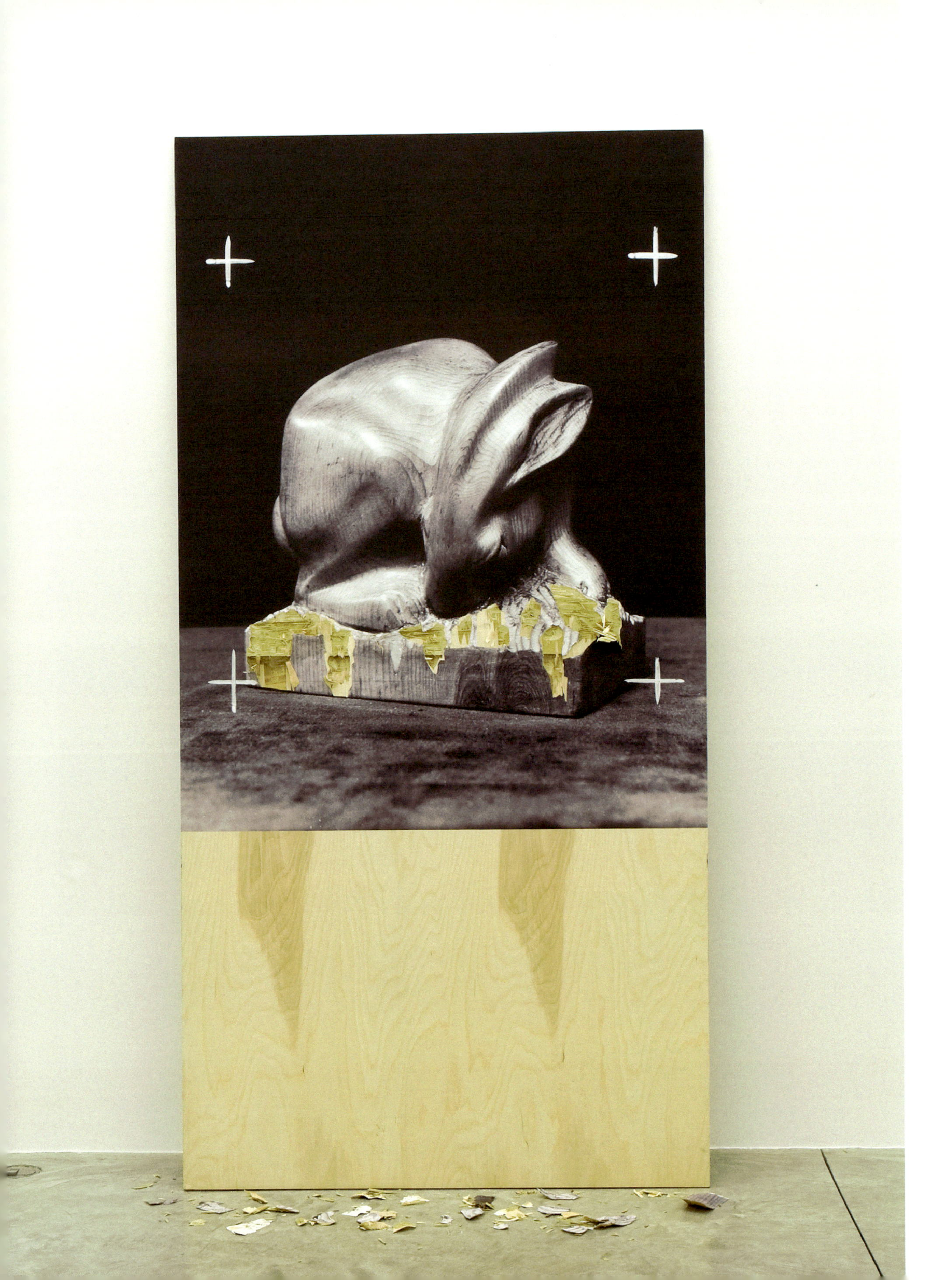

Marlo Pascual
Untitled. 2009
Digital Chromogenic print, wood

MARLO PASCUAL

Marlo Pascual finds her source materials in thrift shops and Ebay auctions, where she looks for vintage pictures evocative of certain genres of photography and reminiscent of a certain era. Pascual gravitates toward still lifes and interiors, portraits, actors' headshots, pin-ups, and nudes made by amateur photographers. These quirky images spark nostalgia or pathos. The small-scale originals are often tattered things that reveal their past use as objects to be held and viewed, then passed on to others in a continuous engagement for a small circle of viewers. Pascual scans and enlarges these shots, shifting scale beyond this level of intimacy. She then alters them further in direct ways—cropping, re-orienting, even bending or penetrating the picture plane. She either inserts the resized, manipulated images into theatrical schemes with props and lighting or uses them as a part of a sculptural assemblage inspired by minimalist forms.

The photo-sculpture set-ups become entities to negotiate both visually and spatially. Works involving a portrait laid on the floor with a rock placed over the subject's face, or a plank leaning against an image and extending to the other side of the gallery, must be navigated around, making contemplation simply a challenge. On the occasion of a 2010 solo exhibition, the artist stated, "social interactions take place more and more with the screen and the virtual, I find that there is a desire for physical interactions and I play with the possibilities and limitations of those interactions."

Pascual's installations are "sites of engagement" where images appear to take on an animated and physical presence. These situations conjure up an alternative reality of images outside of our perception of them and call into question the viewer's role as consumer or possessor of these pictures. If they had an independent agency, they would not need a viewer to determine their meaning or to read them. Instead they act upon us, reinforcing their allure and their sway over our vision.

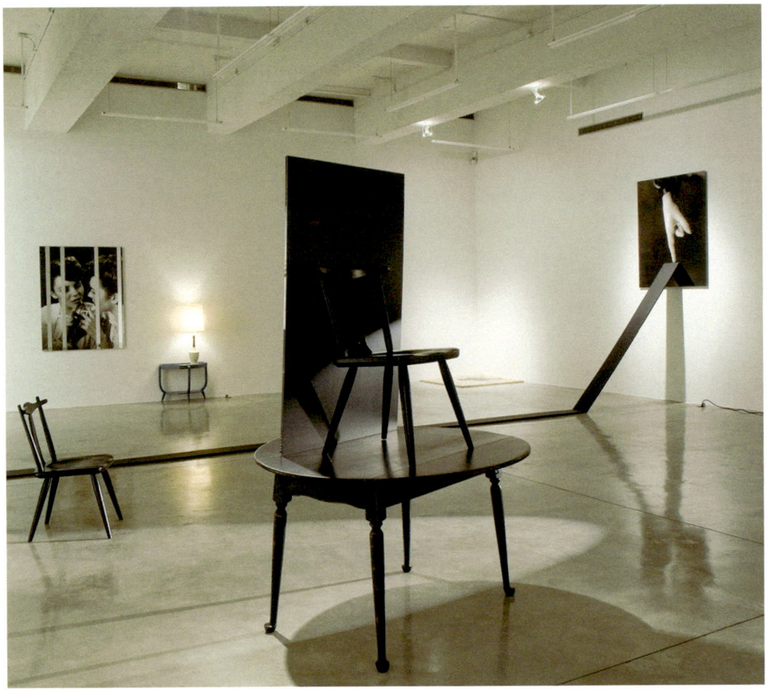

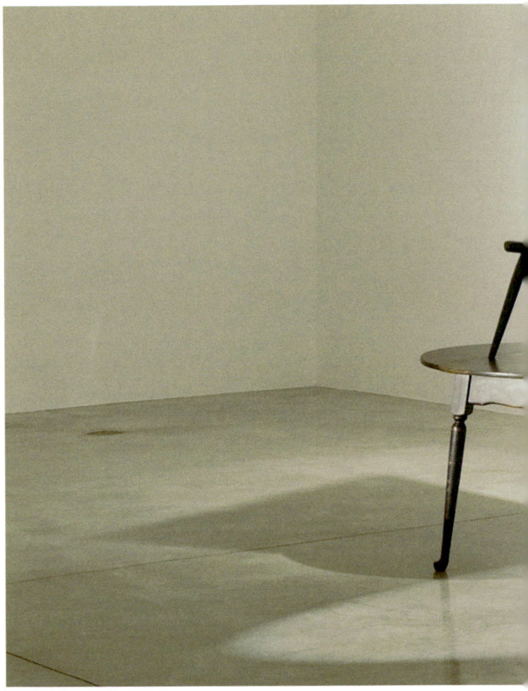

Marlo Pascual creates photo-based sculptures, images, and installations that invite viewers to re-examine their relationship to photographs. Since the first solo exhibition of her work at the Swiss Institute of Contemporary Art in New York (2009), she has had one-person shows at Casey Kaplan in New York and the Aspen Art Museum (both 2010). Living and working in New York, Pascual received an MFA from the Tyler School of Art in 2007 and is a recipient of the Jane and Marc Nathanson Distinguished Artist in Residence at the Aspen Art Museum for 2009-2010. Recent group exhibitions that include her work are In Practice at The Sculpture Center, New York (2009), and Collection of... at White Columns in New York (2009).

left to right:
Marlo Pascual
Exhibition view, Casey Kaplan, NY
January 7–February 13, 2010

Marlo Pascual
Exhibition view, Casey Kaplan, NY
January 7–February 13, 2010

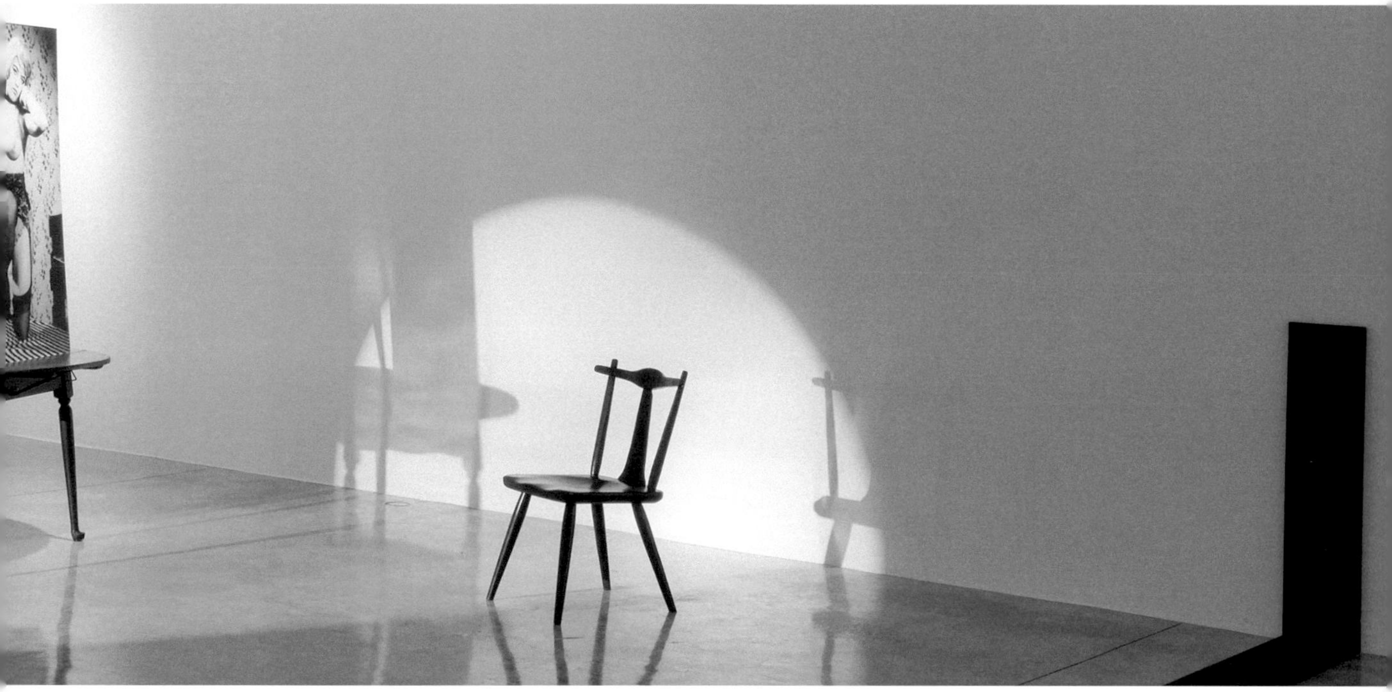

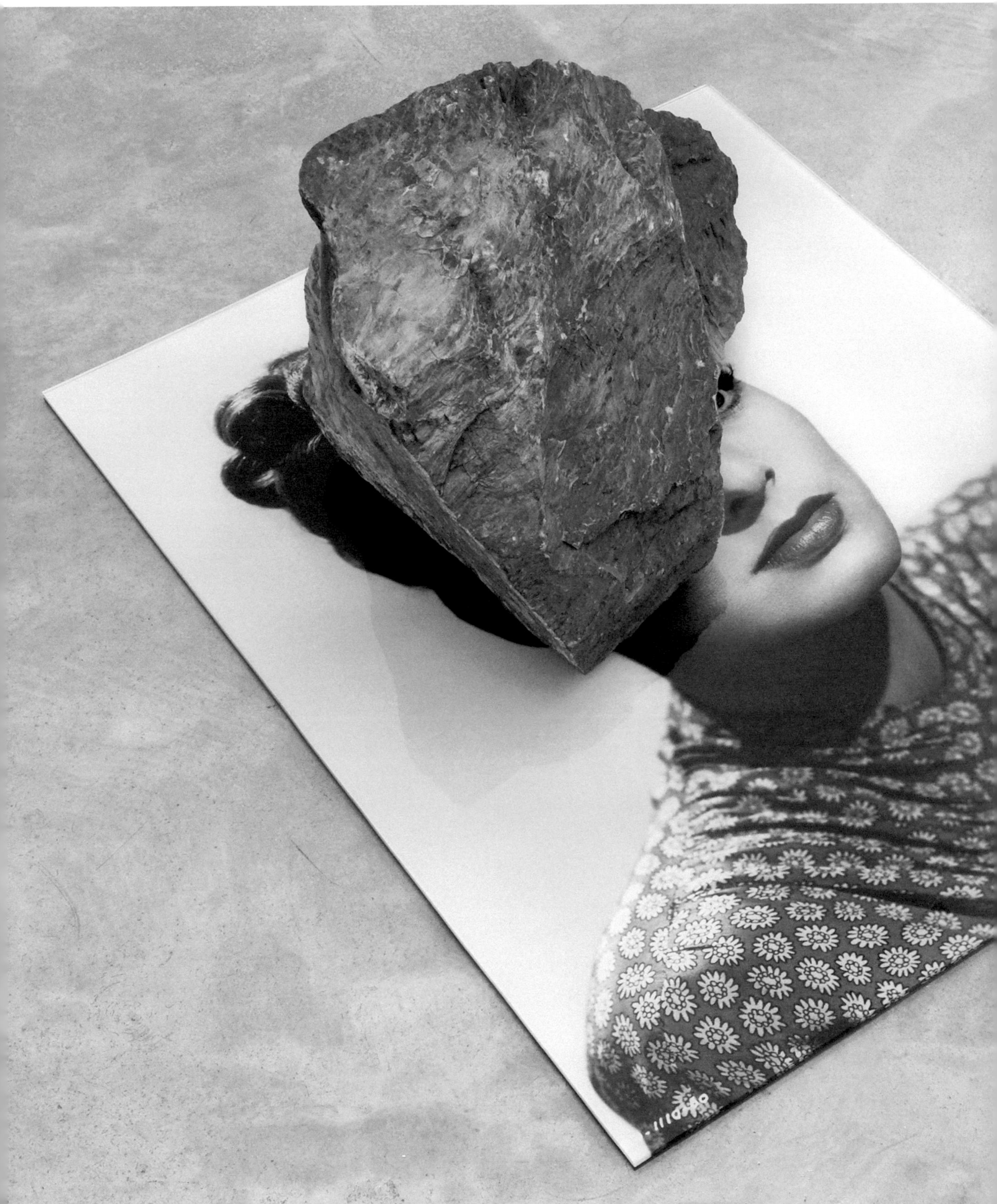

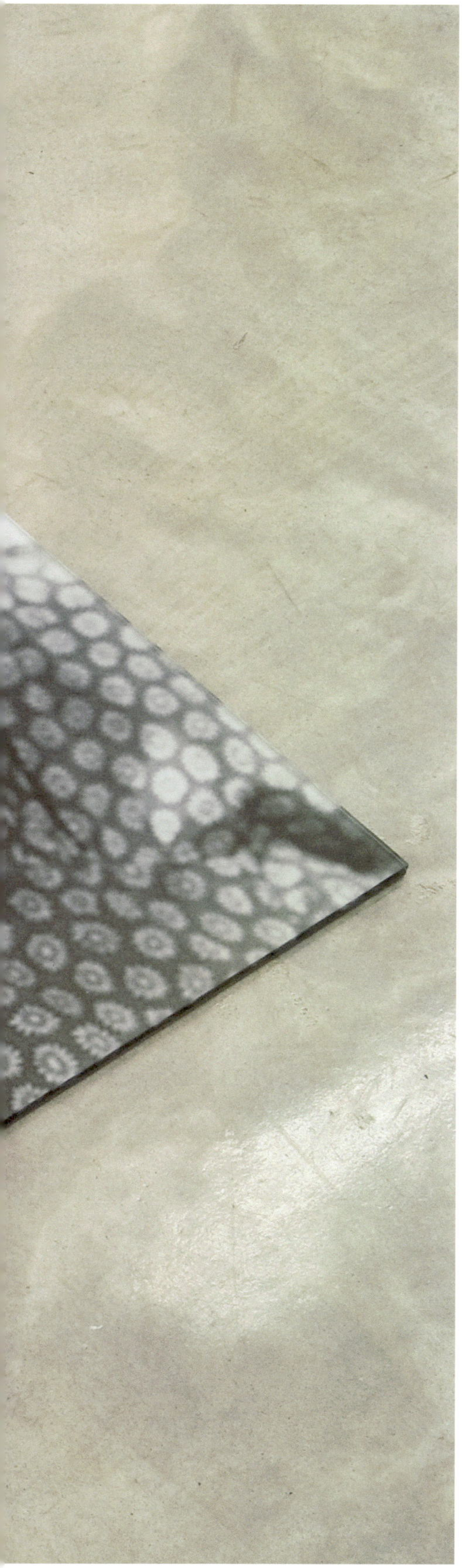

Marlo Pascual
Untitled. 2009
Digital Chromogenic print, rock

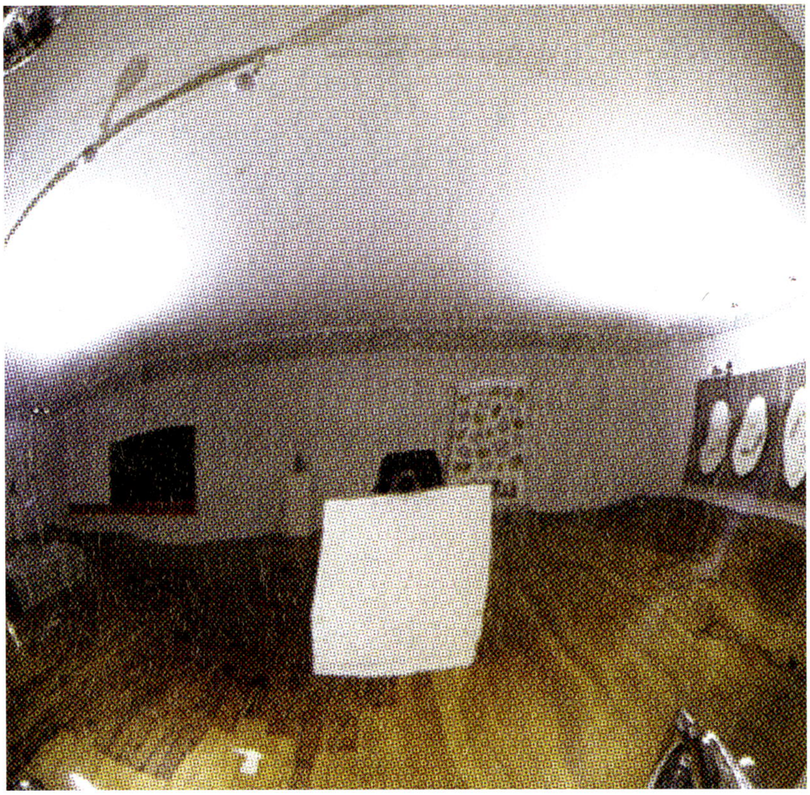

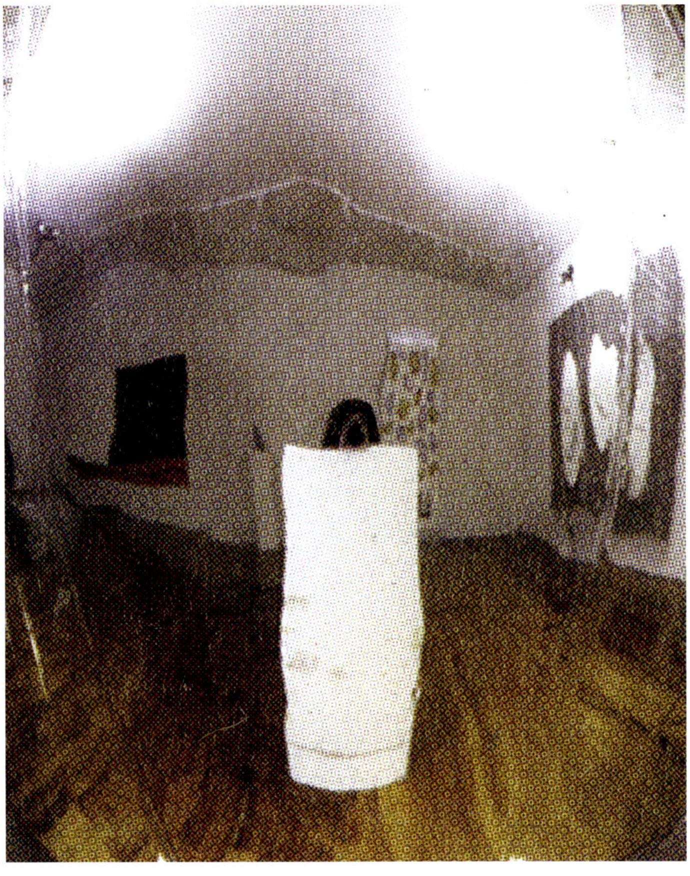

top and bottom:
Amanda Ross-Ho
Camera 1, Camera 2. 2007
Digital Chromogenic prints

AMANDA ROSS-HO

In her multi-faceted practice, Amanda Ross-Ho considers photography through two distinct lenses: as an image-capture process and as an image-reproduction and distribution system. She builds a unique language out of pictures from her own archive as well as from print and online media. Ross-Ho describes her approach to found imagery as "an attempt to locate the personal within the generic. For me, the intersection between these two realms is a potent site for understanding an individual connection to the universe and (to) broadening (one's) perspective." From this starting point, she situates her practice to expand upon commonly held notions of exchange and perception.

Camera 1, Camera 2 derives from a magazine reproduction of Jeff Koons's 1986 polished stainless steel *Rabbit*. The highly mirrored surface of the sculpture reflects its surrounding context, capturing the gallery space it's sited in, peripheral art works, and even the camera used to shoot its picture. Ross-Ho created her images by scanning the magazine page at a high resolution and centralizing the distorted reflections found within the two convex forms of the sculpture. Here, a complex instance of image transfer takes place. The reconfigured space of the gallery and the halftone texture of the magazine page itself are resituated in the flattened proportions of a photo-reproduction. The collapsed layers of optics create a new image that is both forensic and abstract.

Ross-Ho draws parallels between image making and processes of looking. However, this does not always result in the creation of photographs. She understands photography to be a sculptural process in that it contains layers of spatial ordering and dimensionality. A companion work, *Camera (Aerial View)*, enacts in real time what Koons's *Rabbit* also does as it exists in the world, inscribing on its surface a surrounding installation of art works. This metaphorical camera, consisting of a domed security mirror, captures an image but never fixes it. The "camera" here is independent; it does not need a photographer to make a picture. Hung in each gallery of the *Image Transfer* exhibition, these "cameras" reflect and remix the surrounding works, engaging them in a conversation about location and transference that stems from the artist's reactivation of her earlier work *Camera 1, Camera 2.*

By combining personal artifacts and databases of imagery with the residue of studio practice, Amanda Ross-Ho explores the border between public and private in her objects, paintings, installations, and photographs. In 2010 she has had solo shows at Cherry and Martin in Los Angeles and Mitchell-Innes & Nash in New York. Her work was included in New Photography 2010 *at the Museum of Modern Art, New York, and* 2008 California Biennial *at the Orange County Museum of Art. Living and working in Los Angeles, Ross-Ho received an MFA from the University of Southern California in 2006.*

right:
Amanda Ross-Ho
Camera (Aerial View) (details). 2008
Mirrored security dome, canvas on panel

following page:
Amanda Ross-Ho
Camera (Aerial View). 2008
Mirrored security dome, canvas on panel

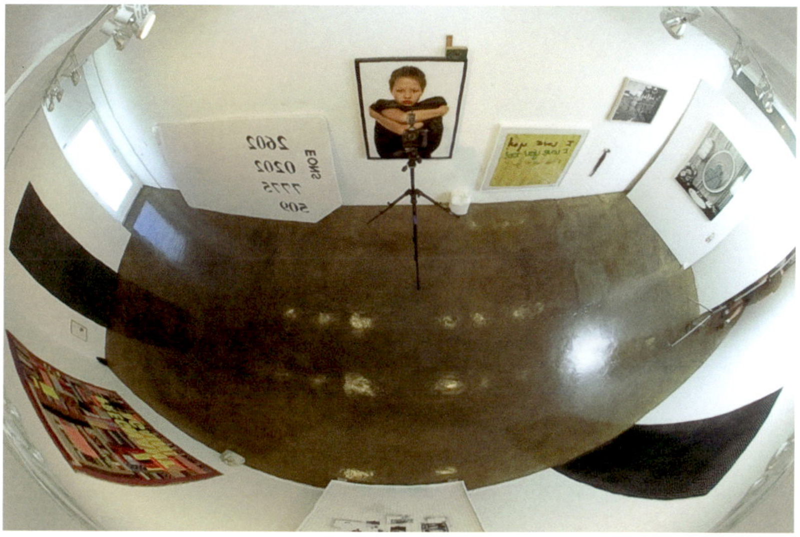

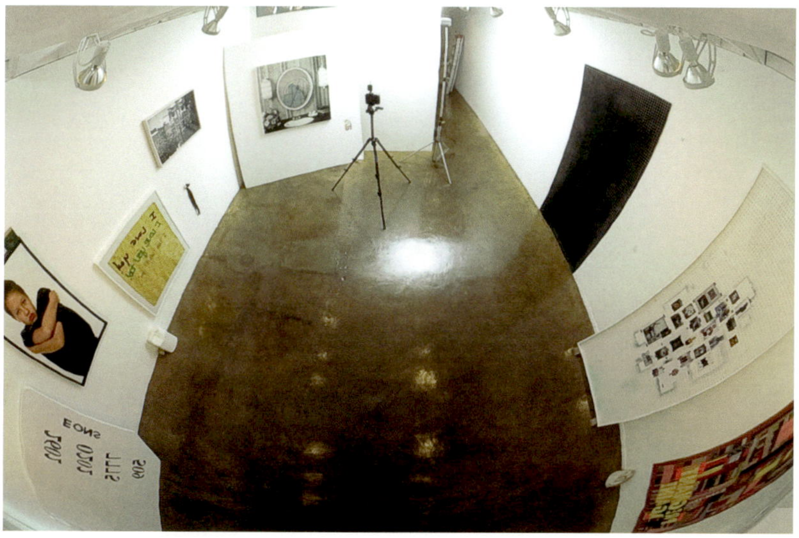

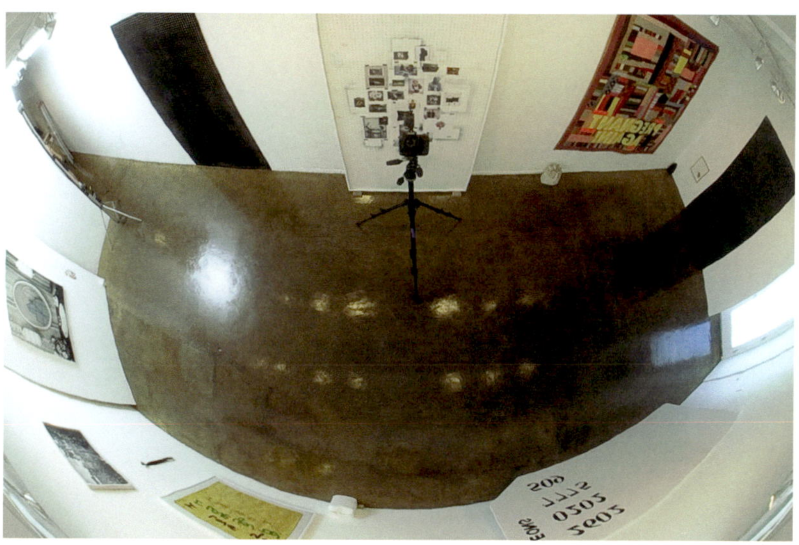

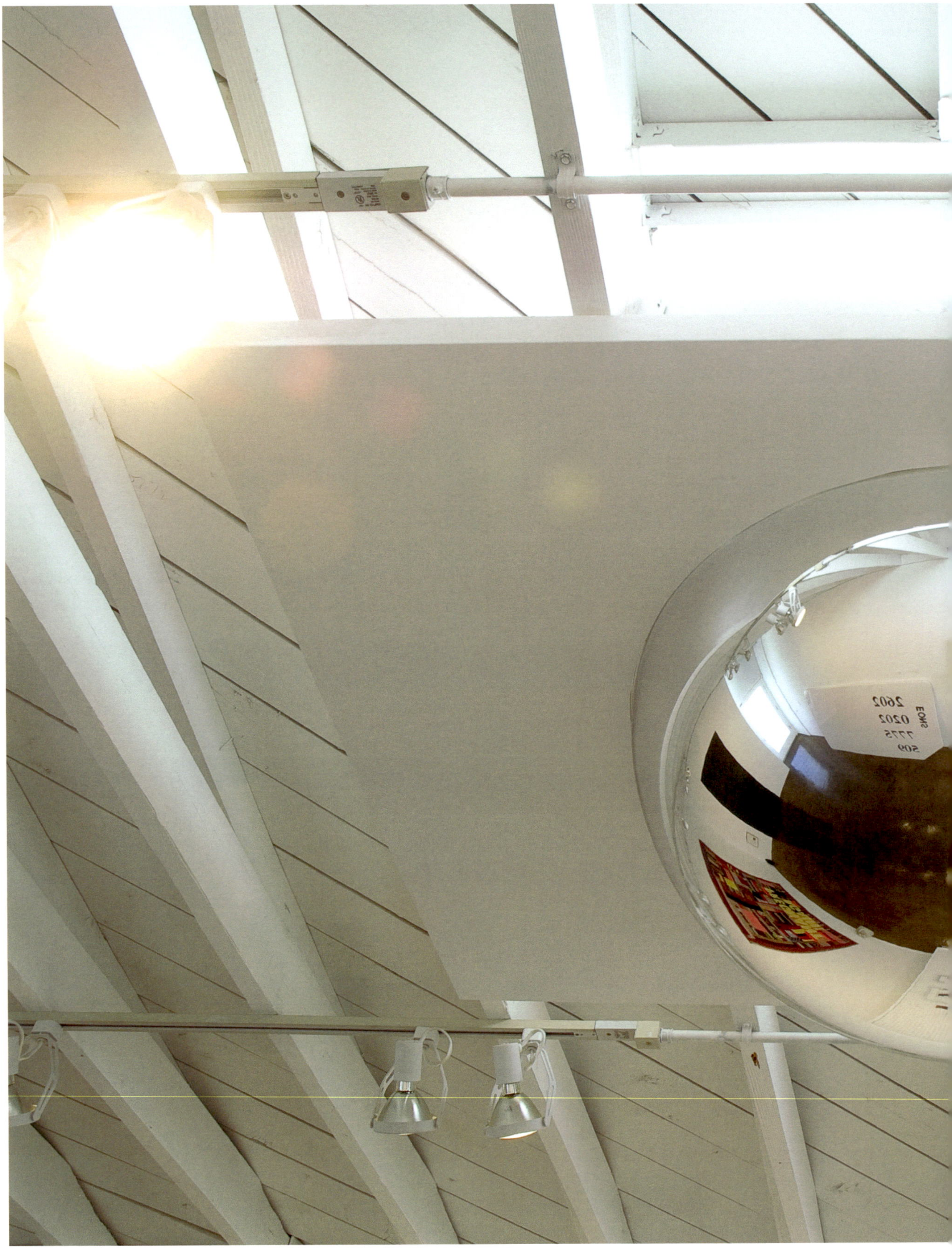

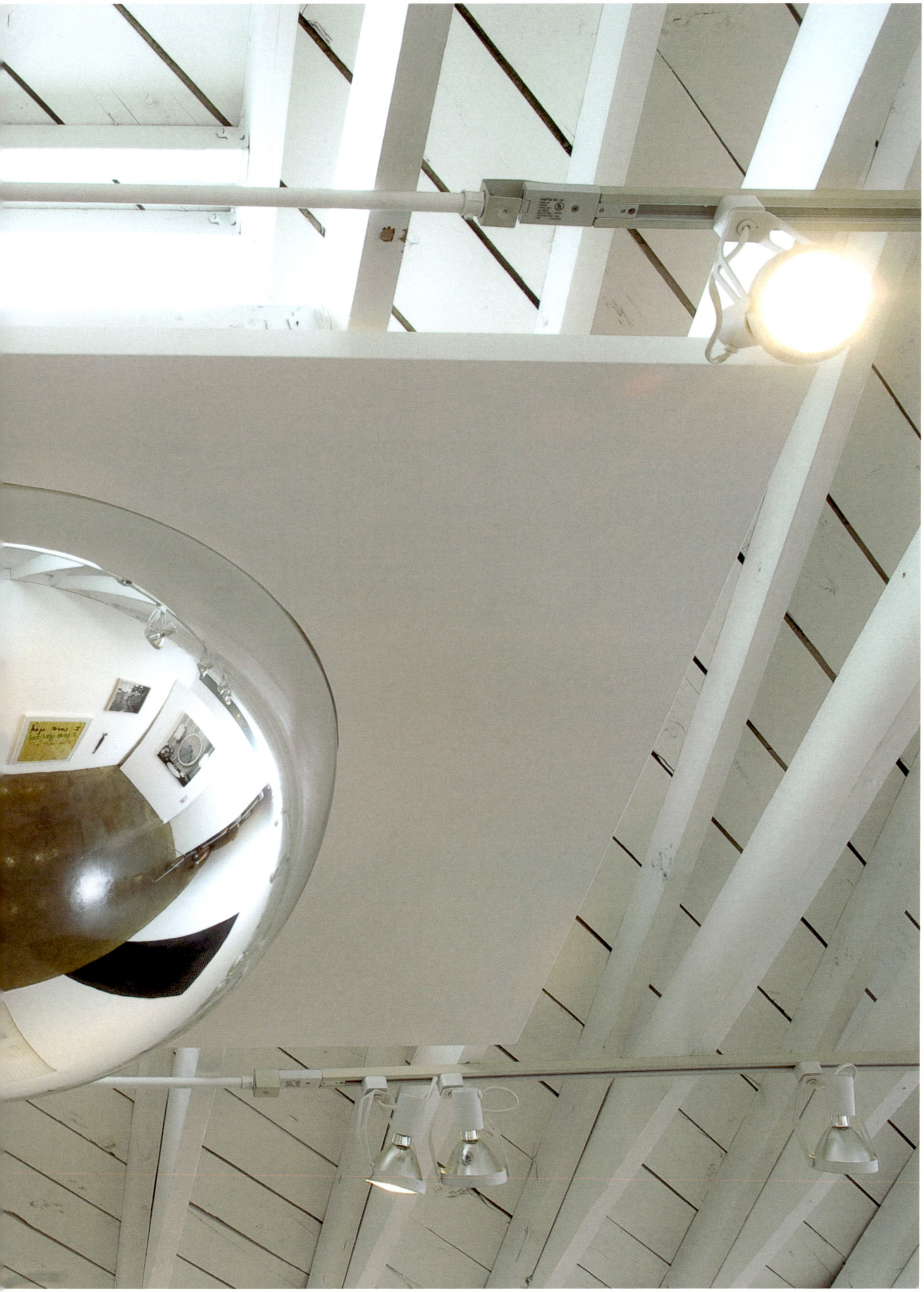

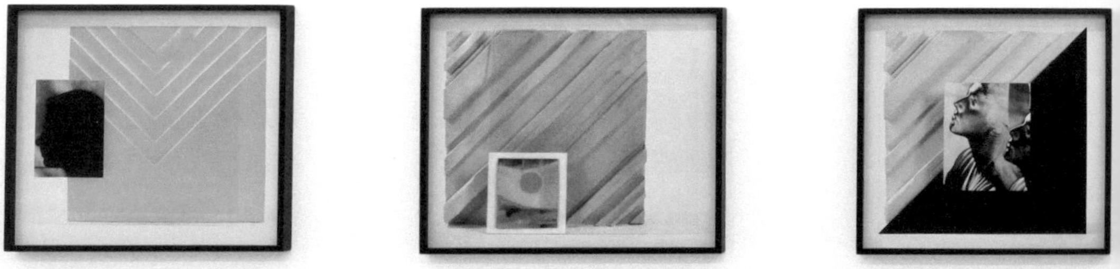

Sara VanDerBeek
Four Photographers. 2008
Six digital Chromogenic prints

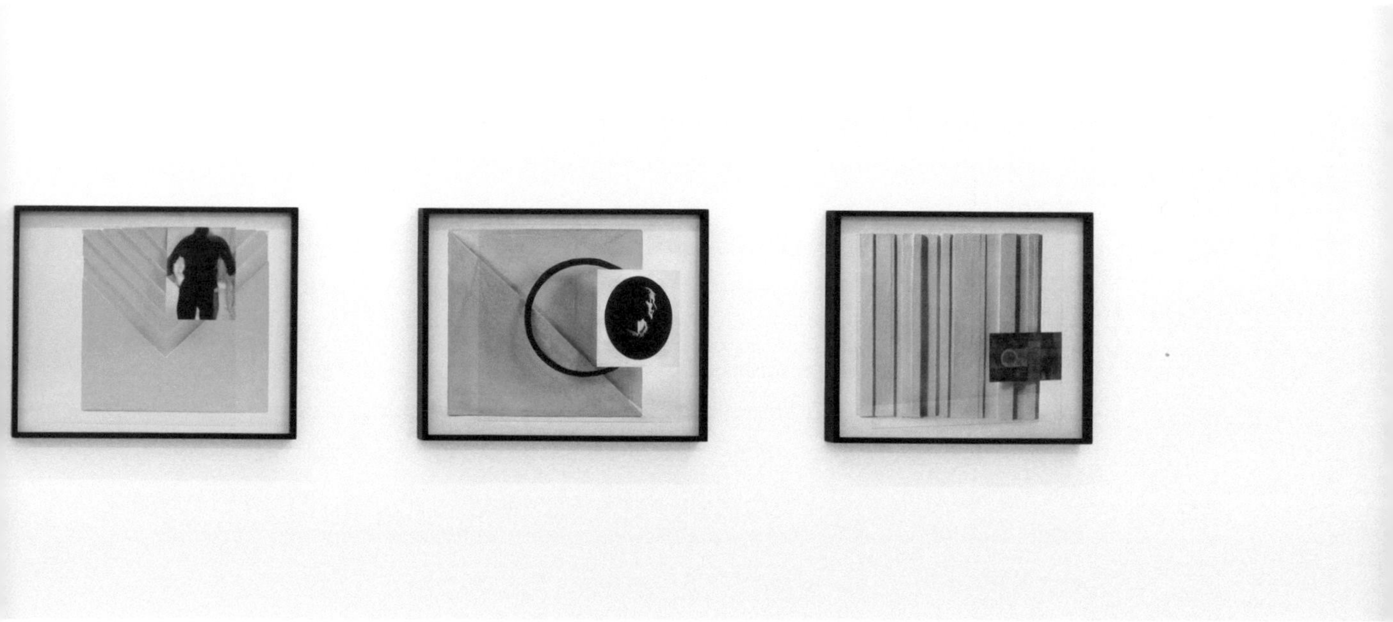

SARA VANDERBEEK

Sara VanDerBeek constructs photographs through sculptural means, often incorporating found or fabricated imagery into the work. VanDerBeek positions these single images in relation to each other; the work's physical structure directs one's eye from image to image. Together the images, either in one single work or through the combination of multiple photographs, function poetically to evoke meditations upon memory, place, and the passing of time.

For each photograph in *Four Photographers*, VanDerBeek made unique plaster casts. She then set glass panels upon each plaster square and placed a photo or photo-reproduction on the face of the glass. The artist arranged both the individual compositions and the overall group specifically to evoke an architectural frieze: in each photograph the darker forms work together to create a visual rhythm that suggests the flow typical of this classical form of sculpture. The sense of movement is also enhanced pictorially through images of dancers. The source images allude to three of the four photographers to which the title refers. Her father, Stan VanDerBeek, shot the image of dancers at the Black Mountain School; there are also two reproductions of abstract paintings he made there. A portrait by Julia Margaret Cameron and a solarized image by Man Ray recall different eras of photography and its continually evolving aesthetic and conceptual aims. VanDerBeek establishes a lineage—as the producer of this work, she is the fourth photographer.

Two recent works, *Caryatid* and *Venus Inverse,* continue the artist's exploration of how photography translates the dimensionality of sculpture, particularly the representation of the female body in various degrees of abstraction and figuration. With *Venus Inverse* this process is amplified by VanDerBeek's choice to present the image in negative and her emphasis on the push and pull between the photo-reproduction of the nude sculpture and the stacked sculptural forms. Obstructing the figure de-centers our experience of the recognizable (though notably fractured) sculpture of Venus and challenges the common hierarchies involved in beholding the human form. Both the sculpture and the image carry forward connotations of past ideals of beauty and how such notions are promoted and discussed from one era to the next.

New York-based artist Sara VanDerBeek addresses the intersection of visual language, photography, sculpture, memory, and knowledge in her studio-based practice. Since earning a B.F.A. from the Cooper Union School of Art and Science in 1998, she has had solo exhibitions at Altman Siegel Gallery (2010) in San Francisco, The Approach (2008) in London, and D'Amelio Terras (2006) in New York. Recent group exhibitions include Form and Photo *at the Museum of Contemporary Art, Los Angeles and* New Photography 2009 *at the Museum of Modern Art, New York. Her photographs are in the collections of the Whitney Museum of American Art, the Museum of Contemporary Art, Los Angeles, the Guggenheim Museum, New York, and the Hirshhorn Museum and Sculpture Garden, Washington, D.C.*

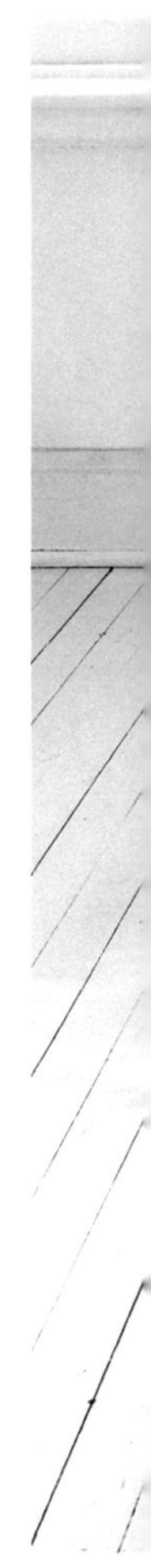

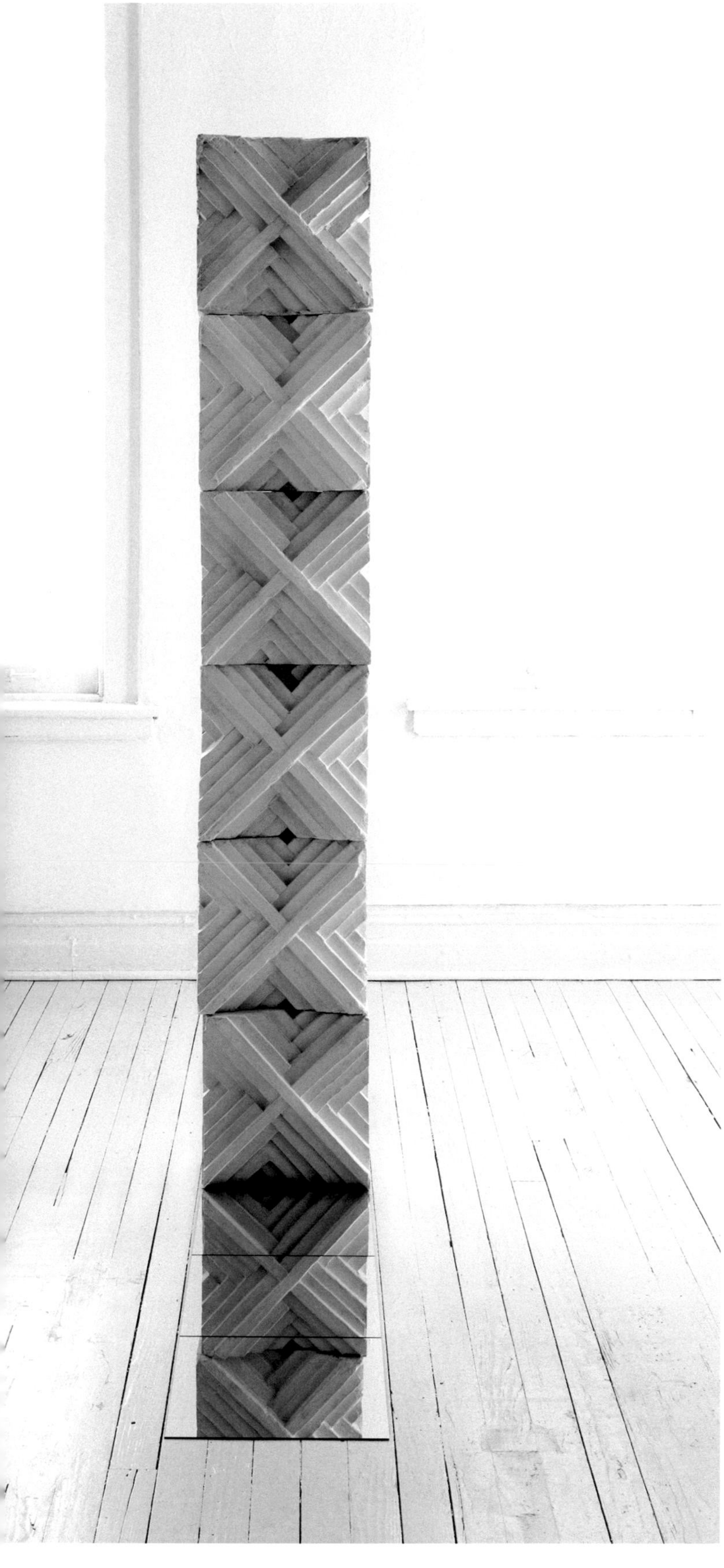

Sara VanDerBeek
Caryatid. 2010
Chromogenic print

Sara VanDerBeek
Venus Inverse. 2010
Chromogenic print

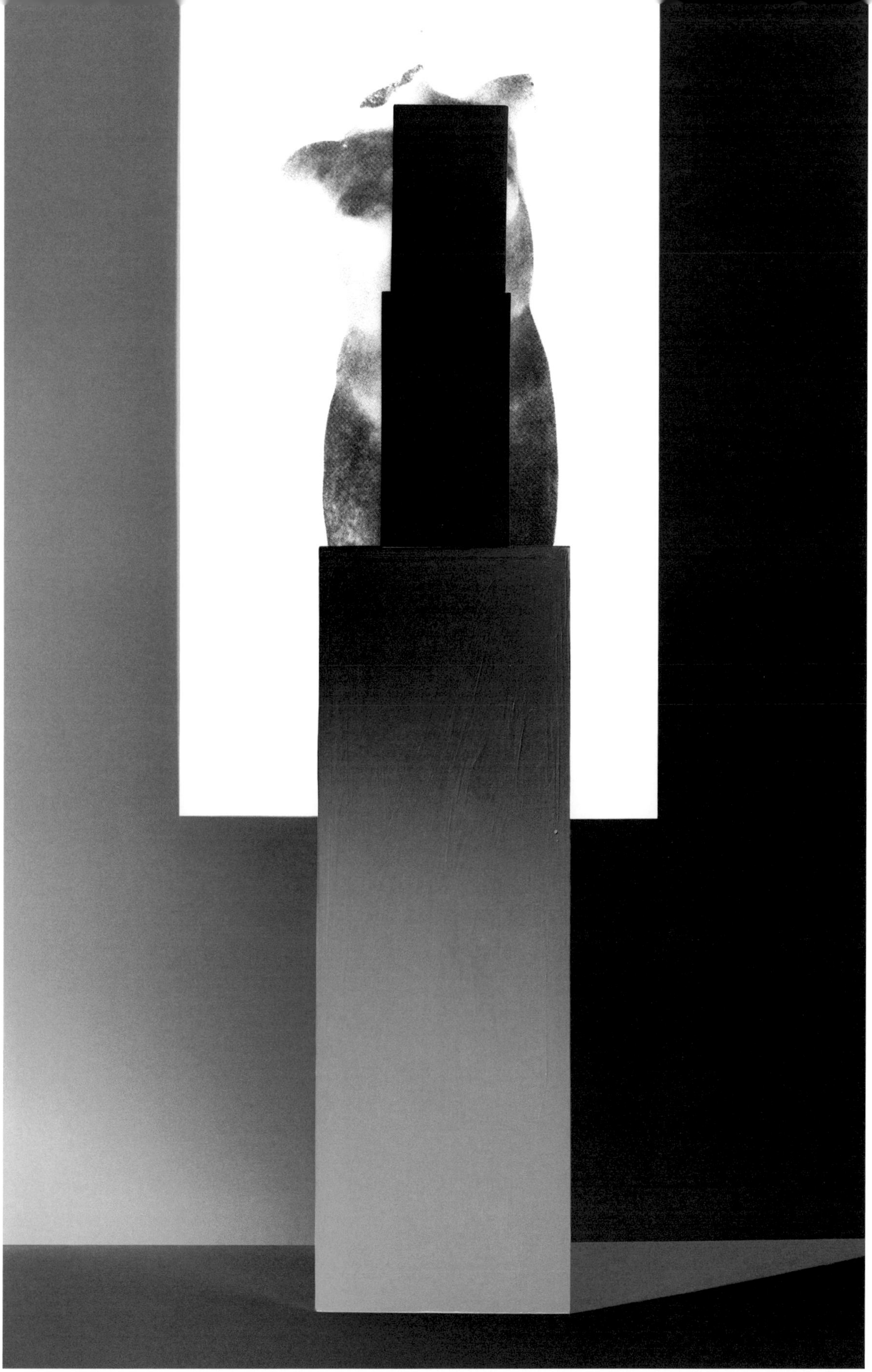

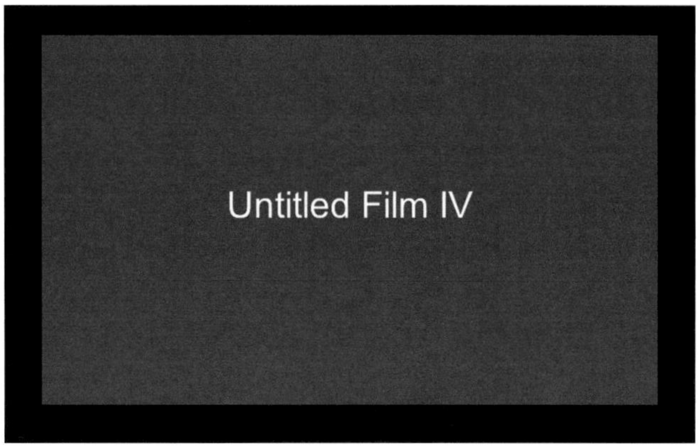
Untitled Film IV

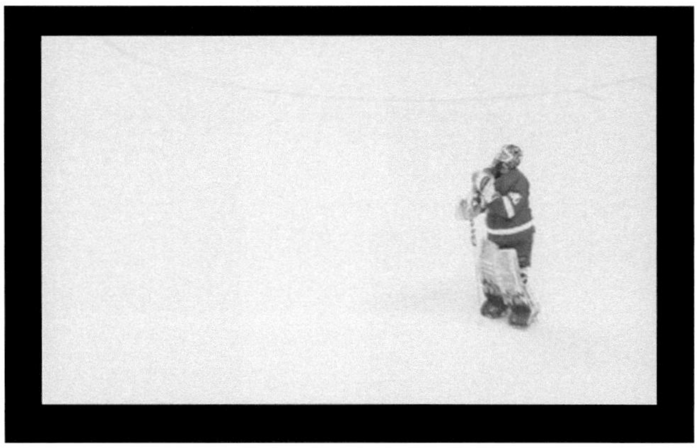

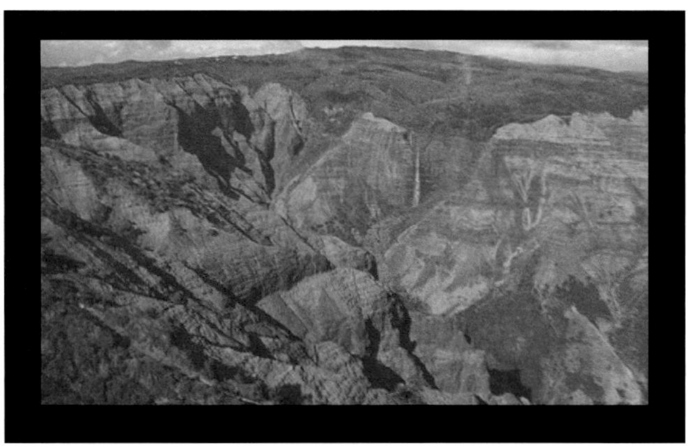

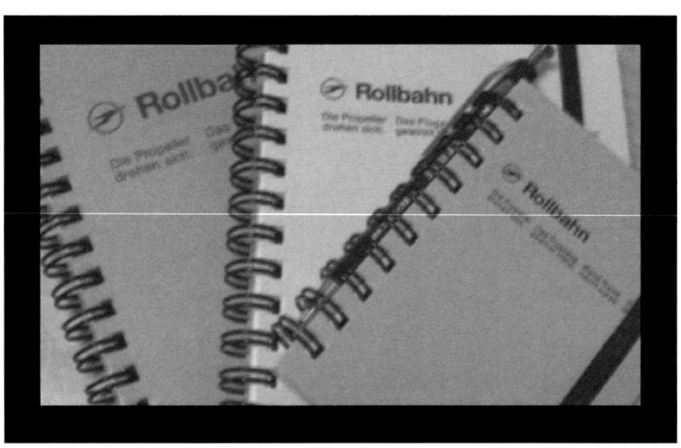
Rollbahn

Siebren Versteeg
Untitled Film IV (stills). 2007
PC, Internet-connected computer program, digital projector, real time random images from Flickr.com

SIEBREN VERSTEEG

To create the live feeds that populate his projections and touch screen monitors, Siebren Versteeg writes computer code that seeks out various types of images latent on the Internet. With *Untitled Film IV*, Versteeg riffs off of Chris Marker's film *La Jetée*, a 1962 science fiction tale told through a montage of still images. In his update to Marker's vision, Versteeg turns to Flickr.com for banal pictures, structuring his code so that these images come and go according to the three transitions Marker used in his film: straight cut, dissolve, and fade. He also appropriates Marker's soundtrack—the audio lends a sense of trajectory to the randomly sequencing projection. *Untitled Film IV* will never tell the same story twice. Versteeg articulates that "rather than a linear structure, I wanted to explore a space where a third dimension of narrative might be possible. Rather than a succession of images along a timeline towards a conclusion, the piece instead seeks a holistic view of the universe—a condition of time where simultaneity is described through the accumulation of any or all narratives." In Marker's film, the protagonist is caught in an endless loop. Narrative time collapses into cyclical repetition when his view from the future clashes with a childhood memory that is revealed to be his own death.

Because there is no necessary connection from image to image, any speculation about connecting threads or potential meaning is entirely subjective. Versteeg's work offers us a choice: we can live with the seduction of the imagined narratives that chance presents or contend with the meta-structure of the program itself. Tension exists between the illusion of the content and the reality of the form but the artist holds out that, perhaps, an opportunity for synthesis can also arise. Exploiting the participatory free culture of Web 2.0 raises critical points. While Versteeg's authorship rests in the code, the artwork that results may be considered a radically open collaboration with an anonymous and unwitting online community. On the one hand, his work suggests a techno-utopian moment of the Internet's hive mind

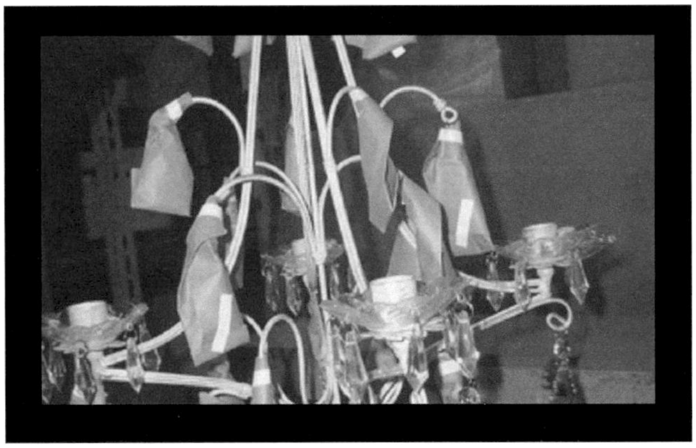

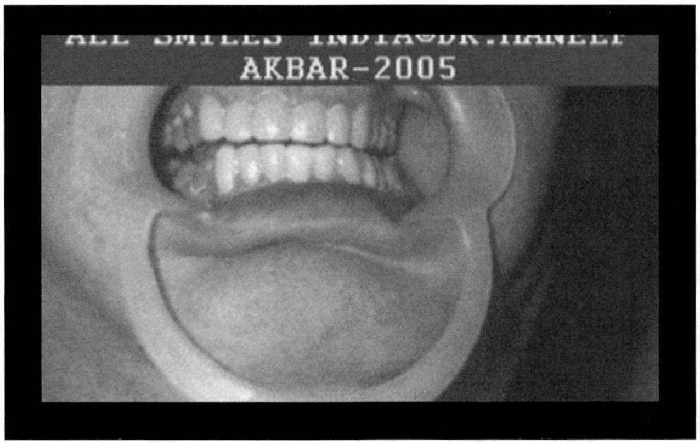

constructing meaning from random chaos. But on the other, it reveals a dystopian view of the virtual world as an overflowing image heap of soon-to-be forgotten, if not eminently forgettable, materials. Will this apparently irrepressible data stream deaden individual creativity and cultural memory or will it transform our understanding of these concepts and our experience of the past and present?

Siebren Versteeg uses computer code, online images, and social media databases to call into question our relationship to the Internet and technology. Recent solo exhibitions of his work are Siebren Versteeg at the Museum of Art of Rhode Island School of Design in 2010 and En Masse at the Art Institute of Boston in 2009. His work has been in the group exhibitions Hide and Seek at Museum of Contemporary Art, Chicago (2010), Mirror Mirror at James Harris Gallery, Seattle (2010), and The Cinema Effect: Illusion, Reality, and the Moving Image at the Hirshhorn Museum, Washington, D.C. (2008).

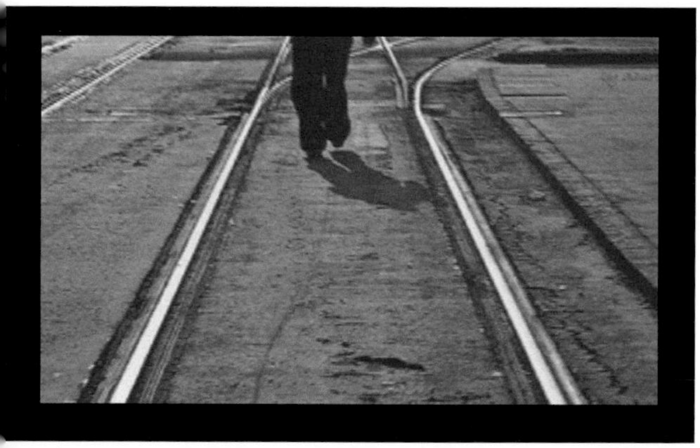

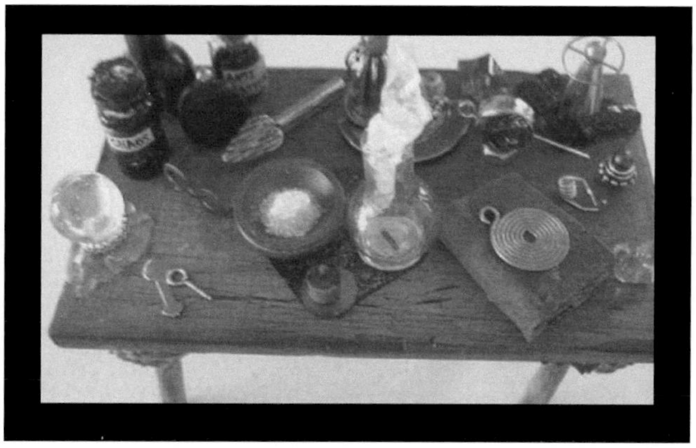

Siebren Versteeg
Untitled Film IV (stills). 2007
PC, Internet-connected computer program, digital projector, real time random images from Flickr.com

following page:
Siebren Versteeg
White Flag (detail). 2007
Clay, fluorescent light, Gicleé on cotton

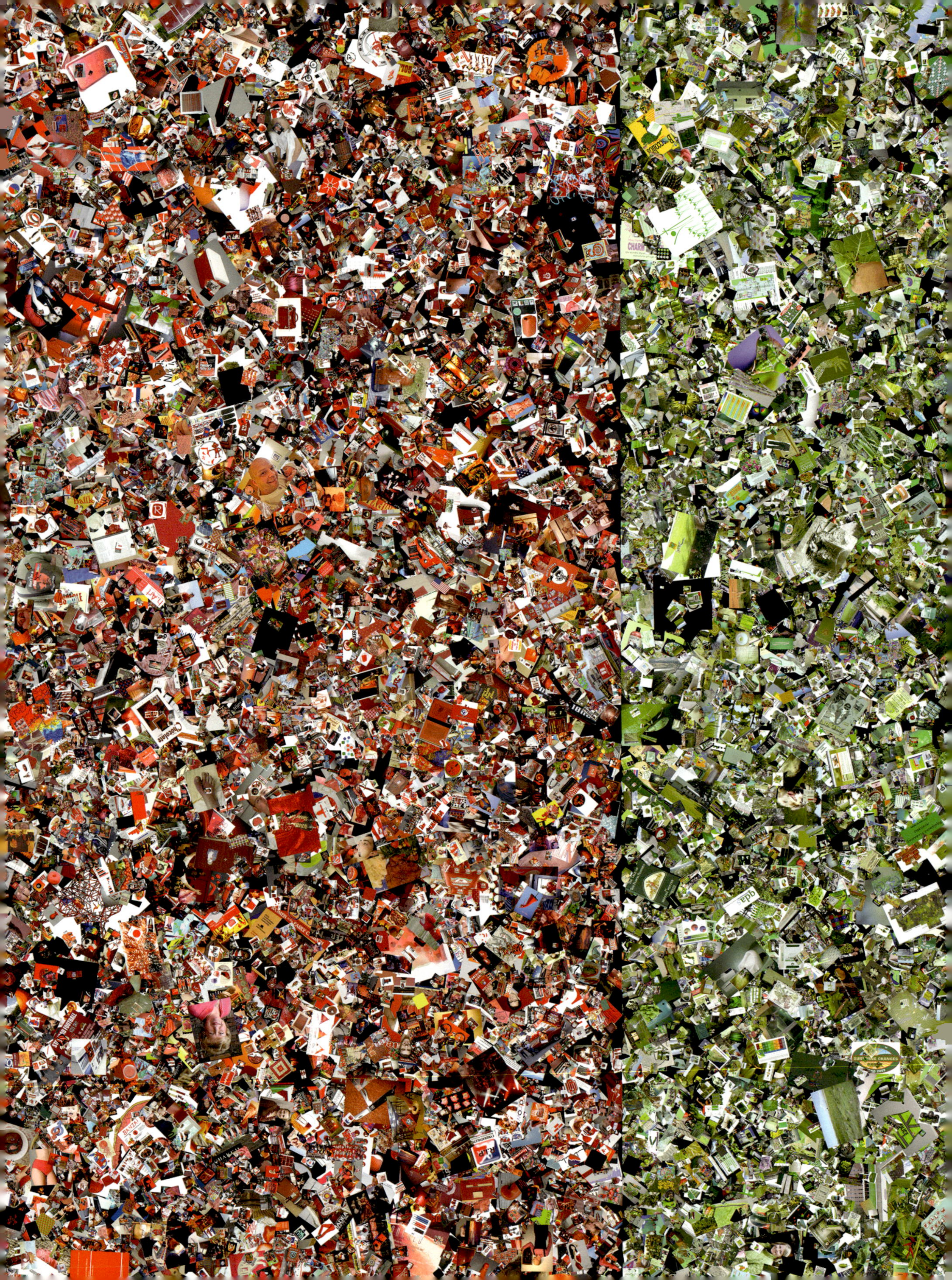

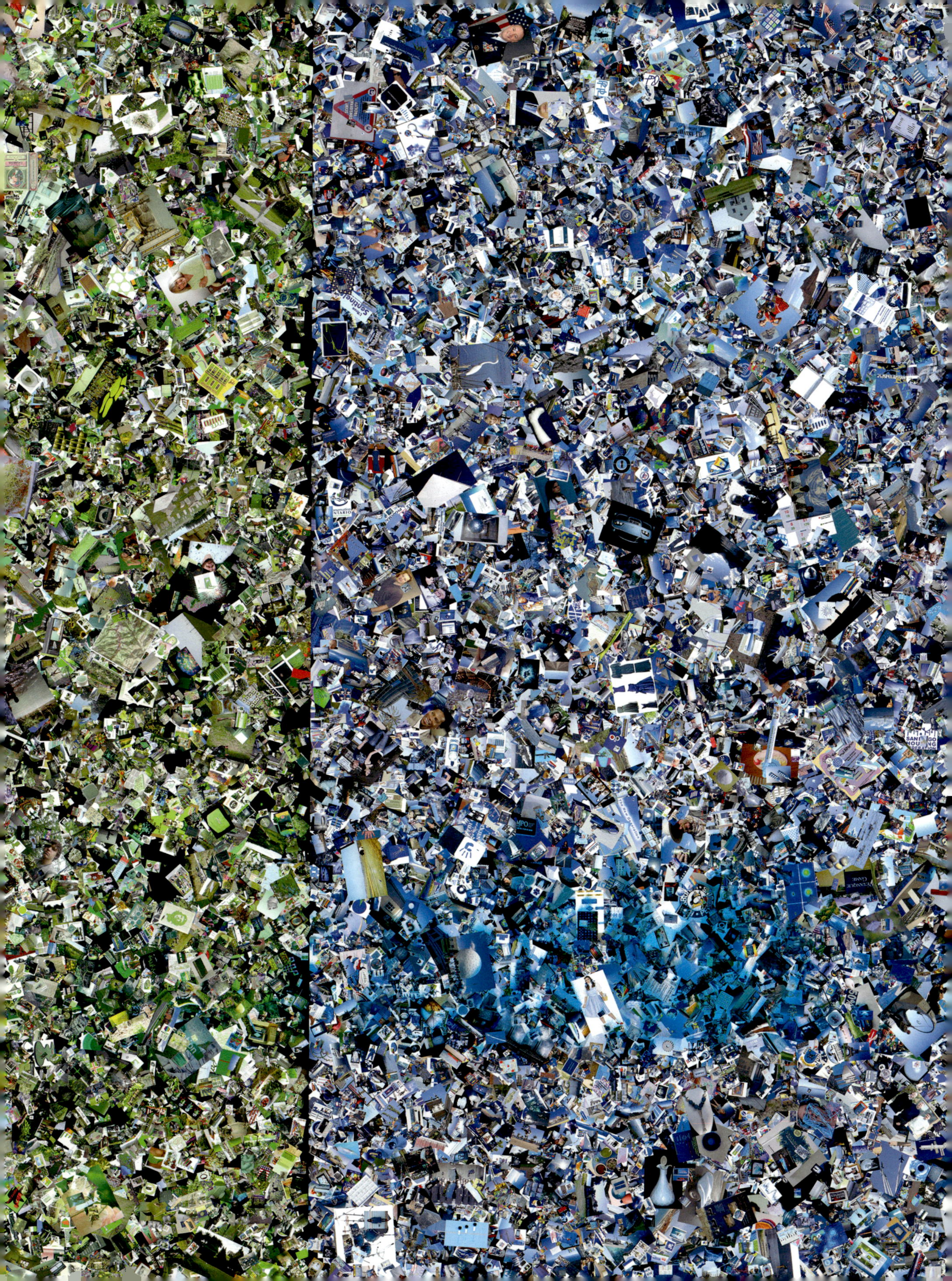

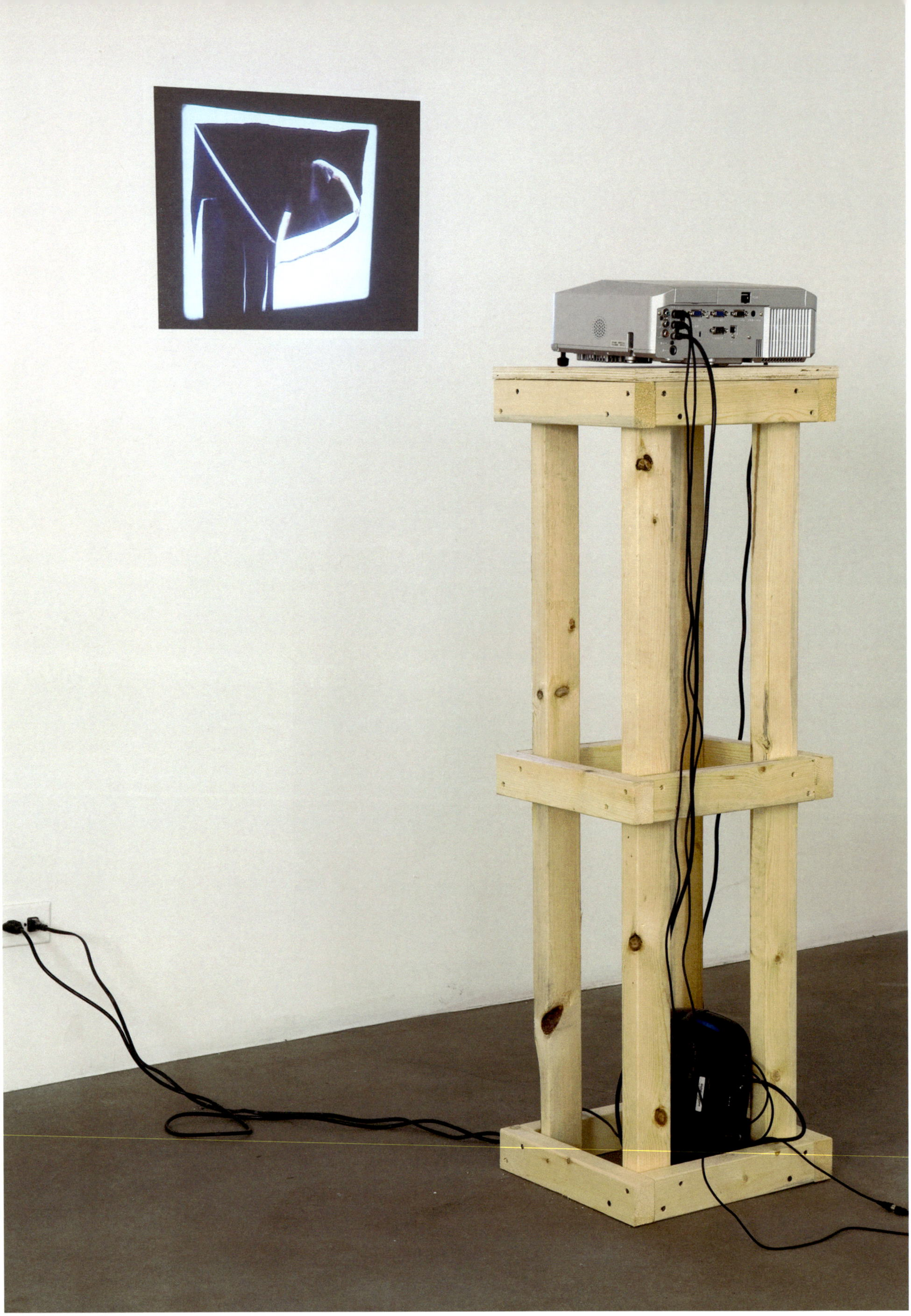

left to right:
Erika Vogt
Motor Post Motor Band Disband
(installation view). 2006–2008
Digital video, wooden stand, painted surface

Erika Vogt
Motor Post Motor Band Disband
(still). 2006–2008
Digital video, wooden stand, painted surface

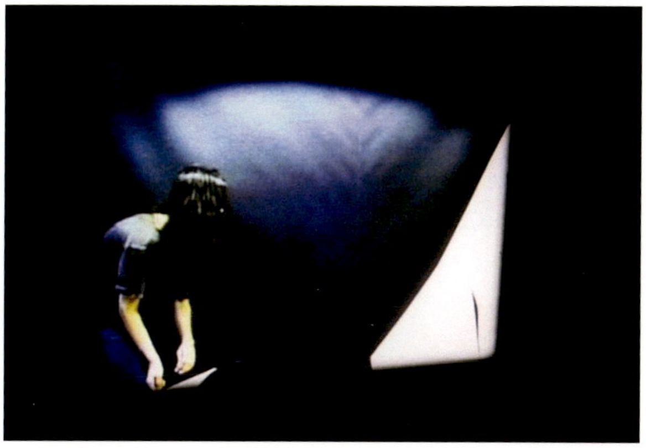

ERIKA VOGT

Drawing on a background in experimental filmmaking, Erika Vogt approaches the reuse of images as pictorial elements to be superimposed upon one another. For a recent group of photographs, Vogt created situations in which a series of interactions took place between the artist and her own image. First she took photographs of herself performing simple activities with distinctive props. She printed these images nearly life-size and placed them in her studio as backdrops for another set of performances with the same props, capturing the action on digital video. The final works, generated as stills from the video, reveal a strange un-mirror-like doubling of her figure in a warped sense of space. For a related work, *Motor Post*

Motor Band Disband, she projected a film composed of footage she made, combined with found video, onto a screening of another 16mm film. All of this was then recorded by a digital video camera and eventually played back in an exhibition space using an inexpensive presentation projector. In both Vogt's photography and video work, various layers of creation, playback, projection, fragmentation, and assemblage serve to animate an image that seems to situate itself simultaneously in multiple physical spaces and moments of time. This method operates like a feedback loop where genesis, process, and outcome are concurrent.

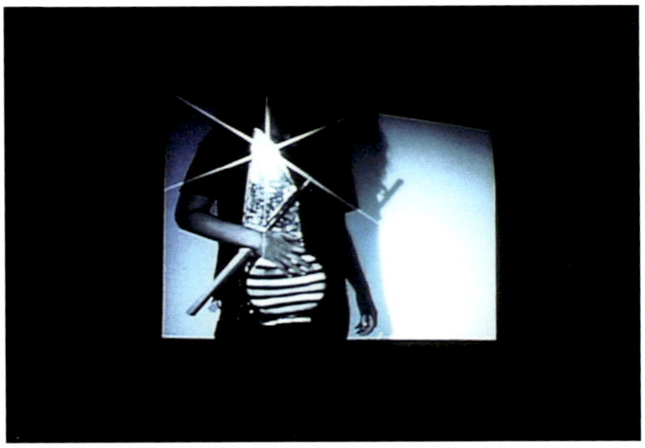

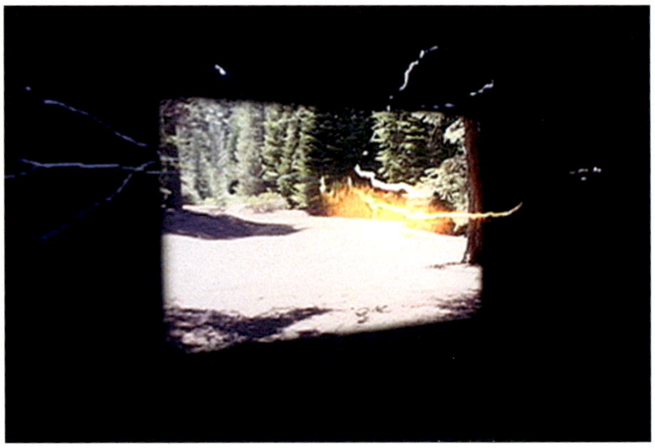

Vogt's exploration of superimposition endows her work with a sense of mystery or magic. This enigmatic tone arises through the many states of "in-between-ness" that her art can inhabit. In any single work, there can be still and moving images, analog and digital technologies, performance and staged photography, abstraction and representation. She challenges the internal logic of these art-making systems by employing a contrary mode of production, for instance attempting to make a sculptural film or a moving photograph. Her use of her own photographed image in relationship to her actual body also places the figure in a similar liminal zone: at once as dematerialized as a ghostly digital image but yet as physically weighty as a real actor. This series of photographs not only changes the parameters of portraiture or representations of the body. It also echoes contemporary feelings of disembodiment through technology.

Erika Vogt
Motor Post Motor Band Disband
(stills). 2006–2008
Digital video, wooden stand, painted surface

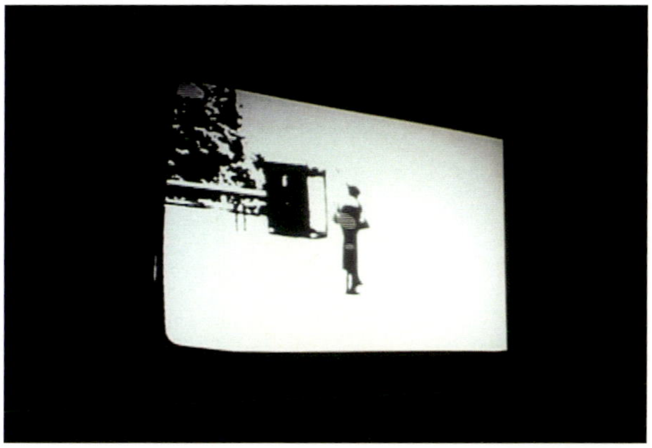

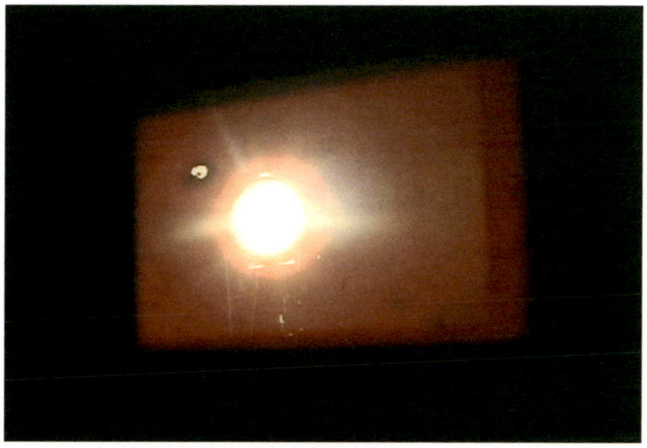

As an experimental filmmaker and photographer, Erika Vogt explores elements of performance, projection, magic, and chance in work that challenges materiality and illusion. Her work has been exhibited extensively in the U.S. and abroad, including Whitney Biennial 2010 and MA at Taxter & Spengemann in New York (2010). In 2008, Mesler & Hug in Los Angeles presented her first solo exhibition entitled Motor Post Motor Band Disband, and in the same year her photography was included in the 2008 California Biennial. Living and working in Los Angeles, Vogt received an MFA in 2003 from the California Institute of Arts.

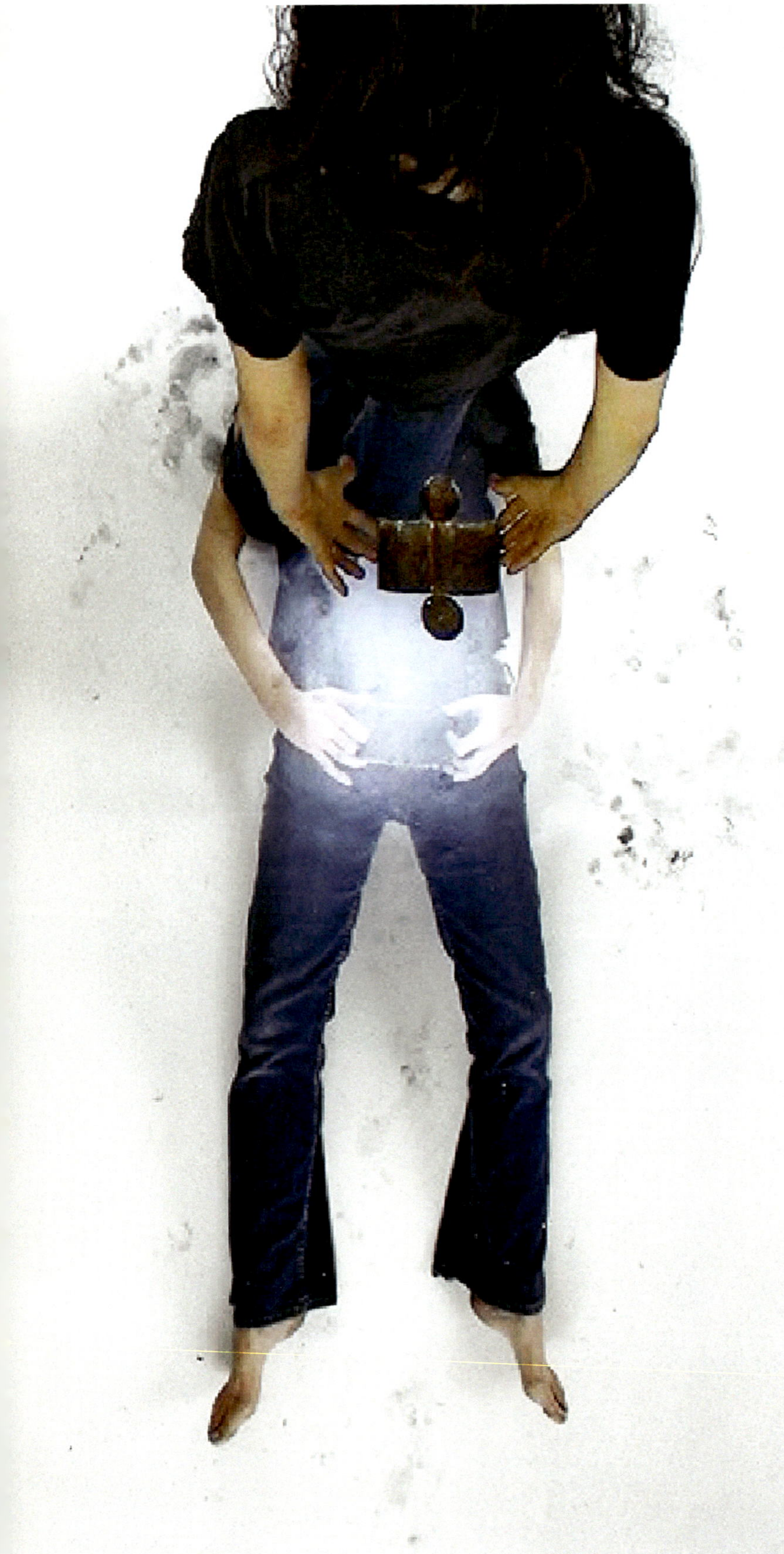

left to right:
Erika Vogt
I arrive when I am foreign (Centennial Tin).
2006
Lightjet Type-C Print

Erika Vogt
I arrive when I am foreign (Mid-century Plywood). 2006
Lightjet Type-C Print

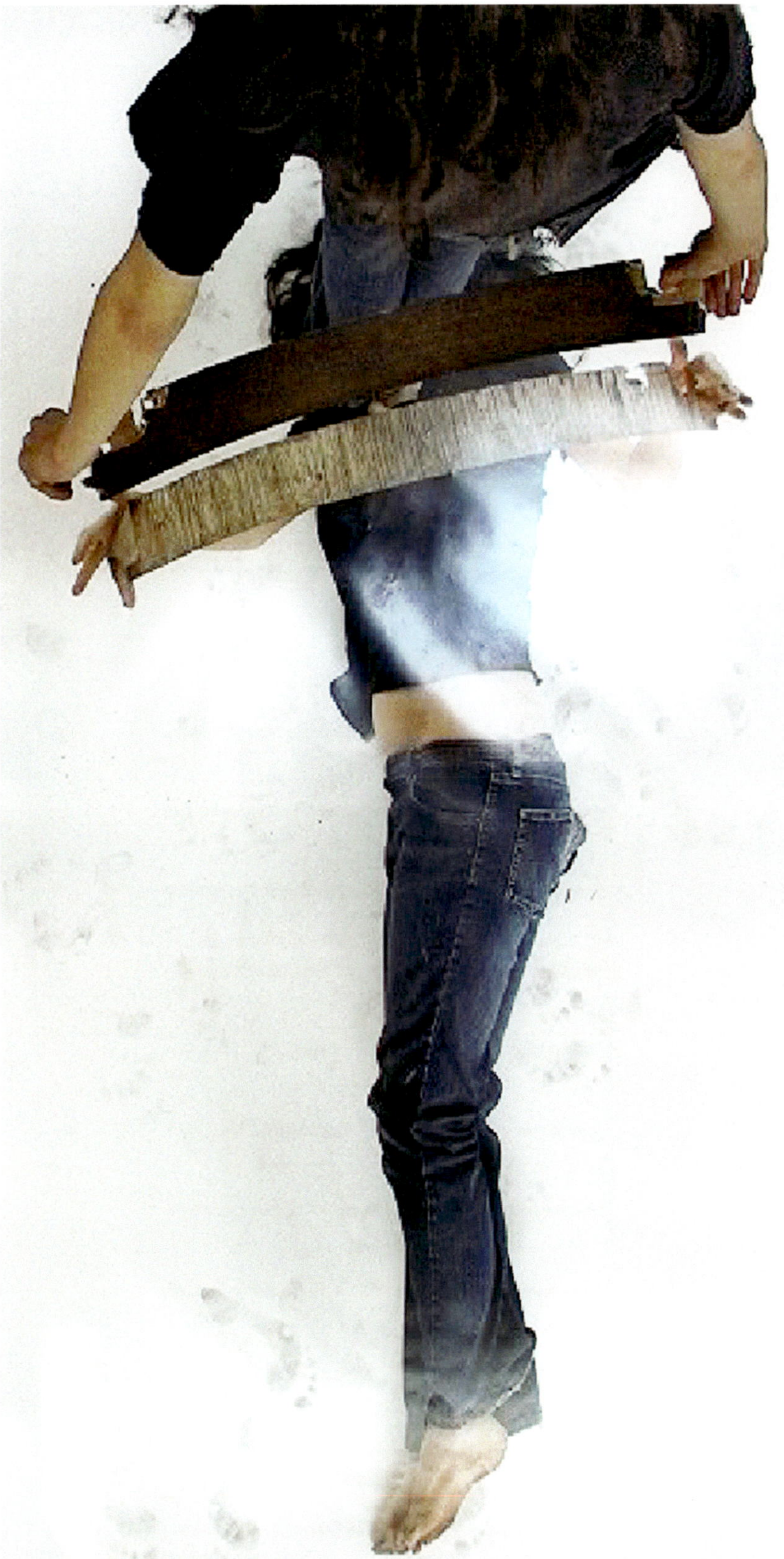

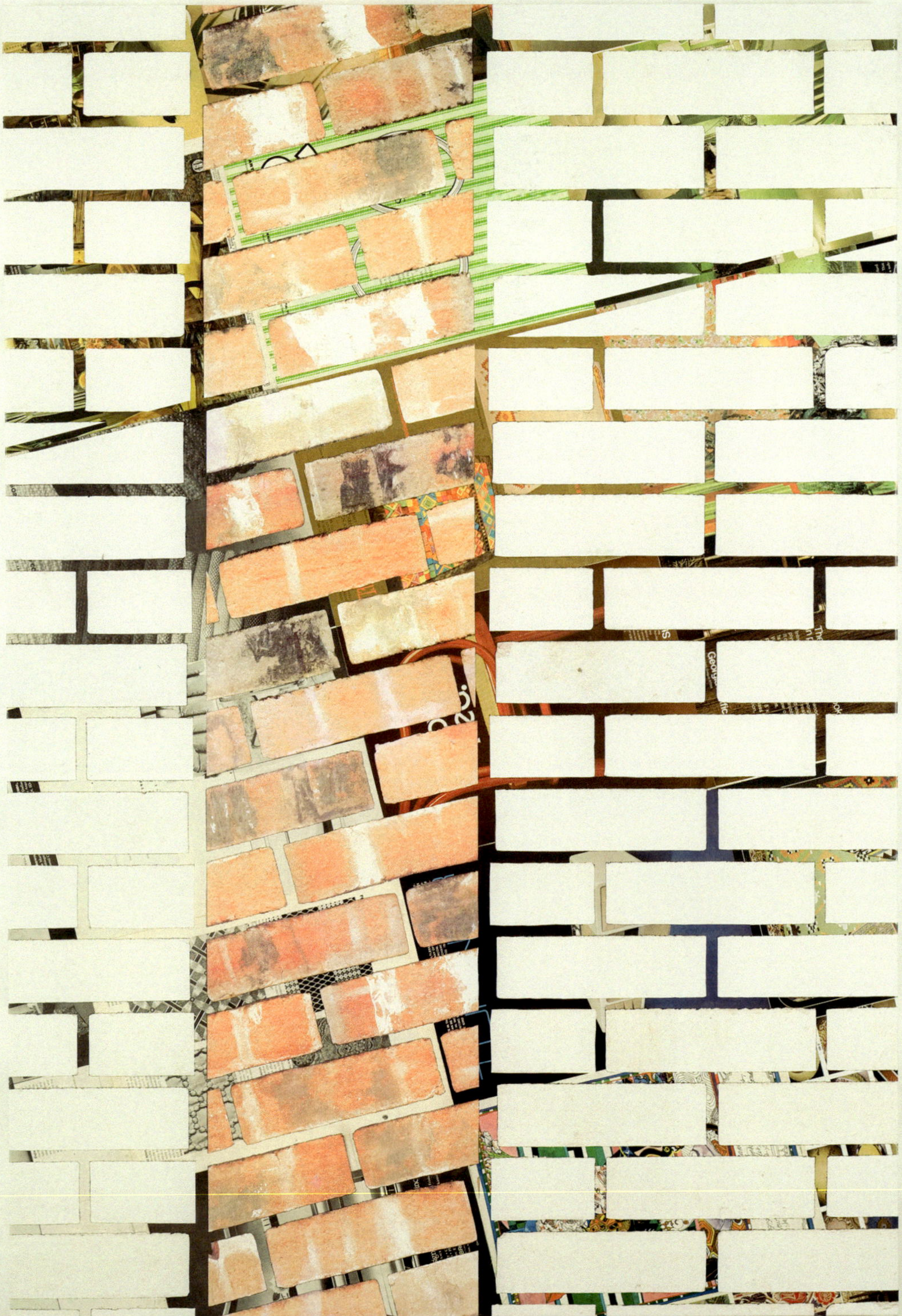

Kelley Walker
Untitled. 2010
Four-color process silkscreen with acrylic ink on canvas, *Penthouse*; December 1973

KELLEY WALKER

Recycling images from advertisements, magazines, and other mass media materials, Kelley Walker diverts both provocative and mundane pictures into unexpected associations. His method involves sampling and altering images, reusing and reappropriating them throughout his body of work. Walker embraces the historical and theoretical connotations of "appropriation," specifically with regard to how images can be employed to establish and maintain hierarchies in our society. In some works, he heightens our awareness of coded imagery by repositioning familiar types of popular images and adding images that he's created on a scanner bed from everyday products like chocolate or toothpaste. In others, he more thoroughly blocks an underlying pictorial source, making it difficult to apprehend the image's meaning.

His editorializing motives reveal subtexts that flirt with the socially unacceptable. A 1960s Braniff Airlines ad featuring Sonny Liston and Andy Warhol has appeared several times in Walker's work in different formats. In a series of posters, the source image of the two pop culture figures is repeated but subjected to various manipulations, such as placing scanned or photoshopped images on top of the ad. Unwrapped bars of white chocolate and dark chocolate are layered in and could be read as a self-conscious joke about Pop Art or as vulgar puns on "eye candy" and lust (not to mention the obvious racial joke).

Walker uses his scanner quite prodigiously. For an ongoing series of paintings, he silk-screens images of scanned bricks onto canvas. Paired with the bricks is a specific issue of a popular magazine, like *Time* or *Hustler* of vintage dates that evoke a particular genre and era. What is visible and what is concealed is left largely to chance; the paintings don't relate much to their pulp journalism content beyond what is conjured in the viewer's imagination. Walker complicates our perception by applying the bricks to the support first and then placing the magazine pages as if they were mortar around the simulated bricks. Scott Rothkopf writes in his

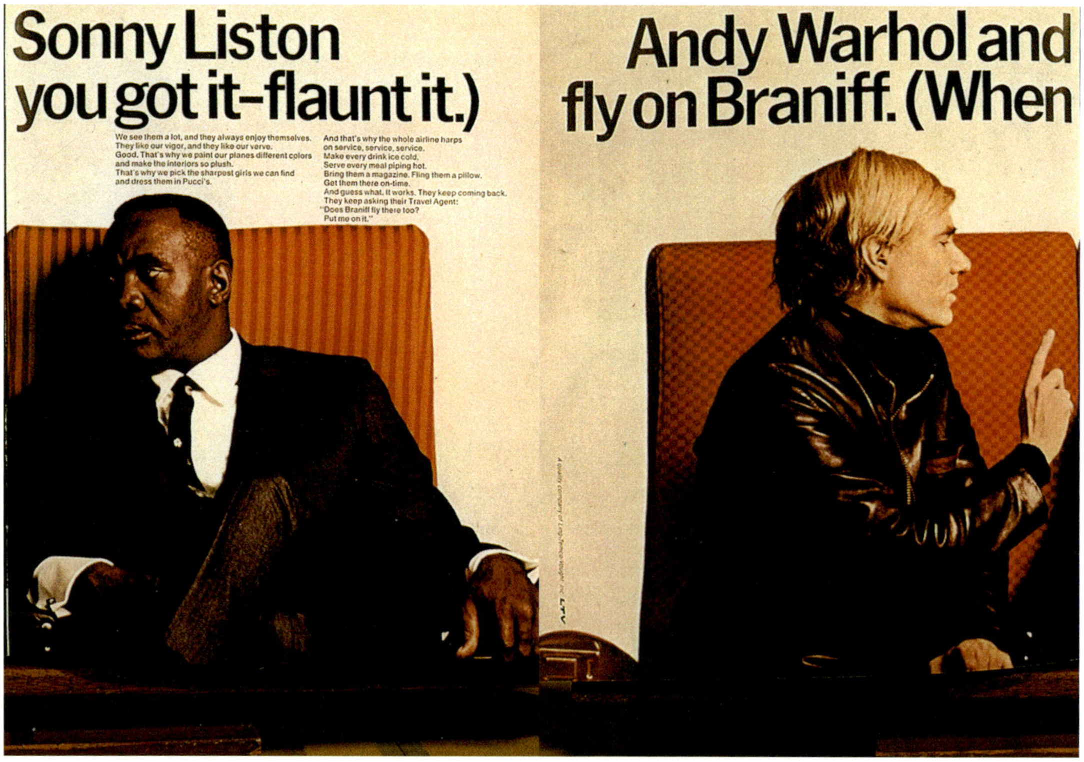

2008 monograph on the artist, "these paintings have a surreal, almost hallucinatory presence, at once extremely painterly yet hyper-photographic. Each brick seems to jump off the surface in bold relief, while the variation in their hues, from citron to mauve, makes them look somehow like bad color reproductions of themselves, which to a certain extent, they are."

Kelley Walker's work provocatively appropriates cultural icons to comment on issues of politics and consumerism. Walker alters these images through scanning, silkscreen, and other media to investigate issues of circulation, reproduction, and re-appropriation in the digital age. His work has been exhibited widely in many national and international venues over the last decade. Recent solo exhibitions include the Thomas Dane Gallery in London (2010) and Capitain Petzel Gallery in Berlin (2009); and group exhibitions Collage: The Unmonumental Picture (2007) at the New Museum and Beg, Borrow, and Steal at the Rubell Family Collection, Miami (2009). Walker also works and exhibits collaboratively with Wade Guyton as Guyton/Walker.

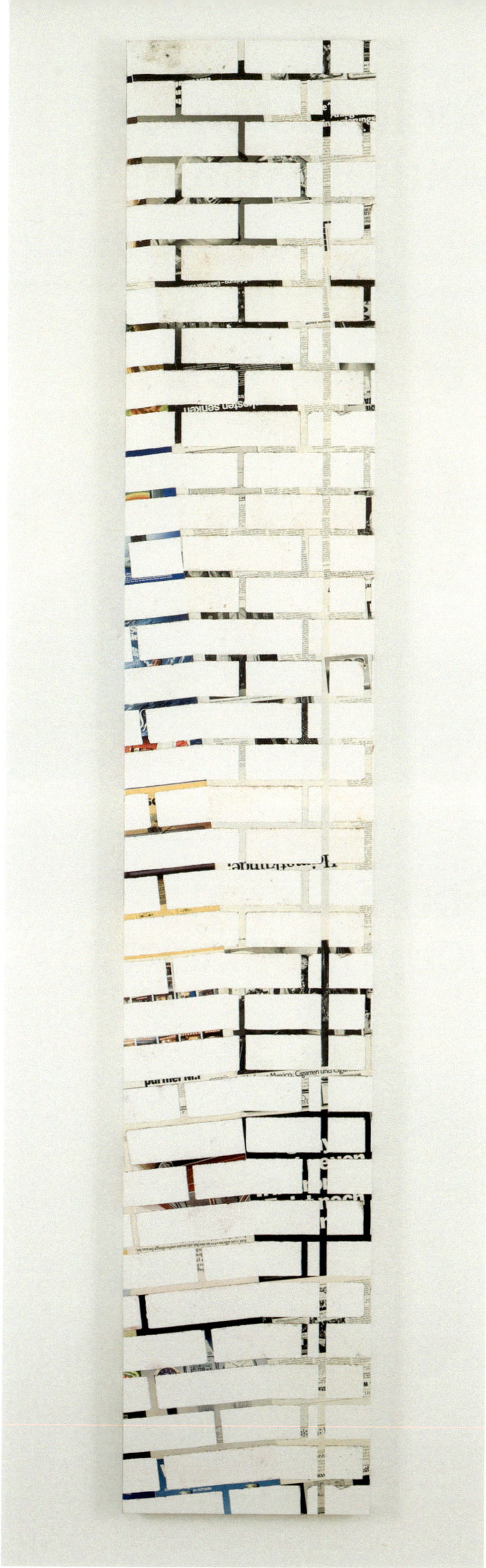

left to right:
Kelley Walker
Andy Warhol and Sonny Liston Fly on Braniff (When you got it-flaunt it) (detail).
2005–2007
3 offset color posters

Kelley Walker
Untitled. 2010
Four-color process silkscreen with acrylic ink on canvas, *Der Speigel*; December 1973.

following pages:
Kelley Walker
Andy Warhol and Sonny Liston Fly on Braniff (When you got it-flaunt it) (details).
2005–2007
3 offset color posters

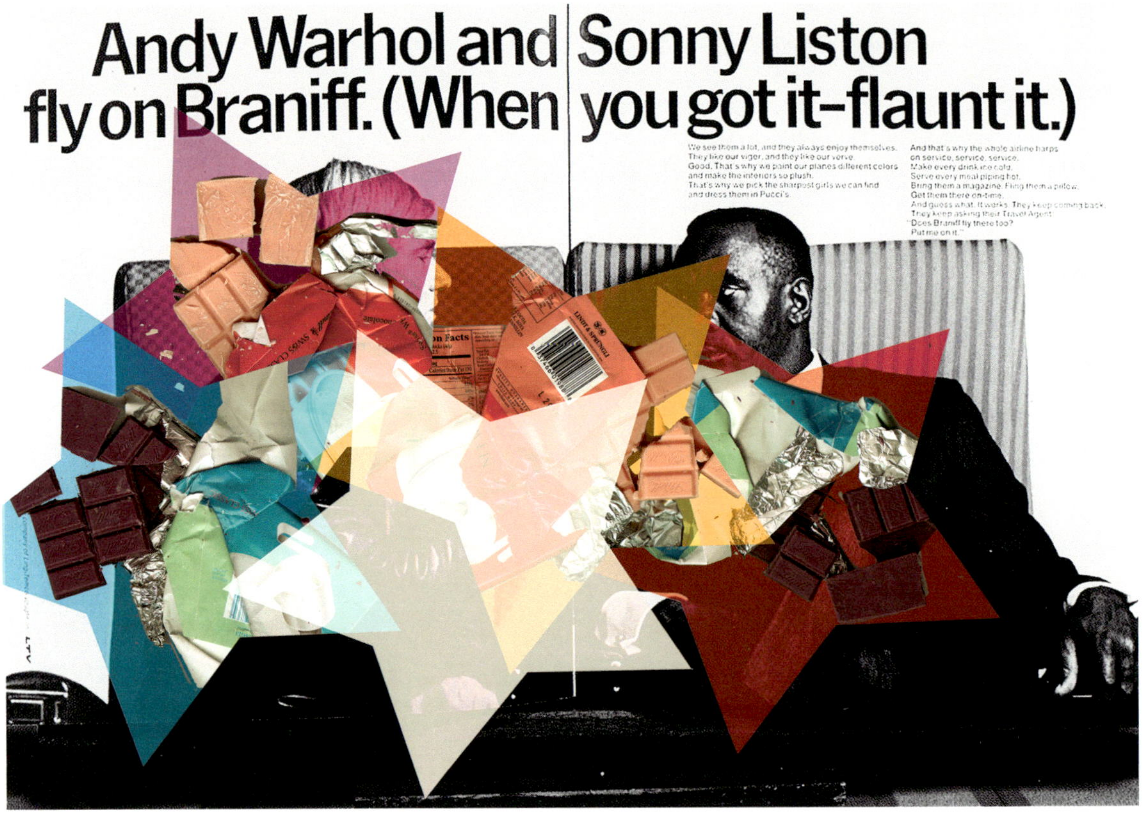
Andy Warhol and Sonny Liston fly on Braniff. (When you got it–flaunt it.)
We see them a lot, and they always enjoy themselves. They like our vigor, and they like our verve. Good. That's why we paint our planes different colors and make the interiors so plush. That's why we pick the sharpest girls we can find and dress them in Pucci's.
And that's why the whole airline harps on service, service, service. Make every drink ice cold. Serve every meal piping hot. Bring them a magazine. Fling them a pillow. Get them there on-time. And guess what. It works. They keep coming back. They keep asking their Travel Agent: "Does Braniff fly there too? Put me on it."

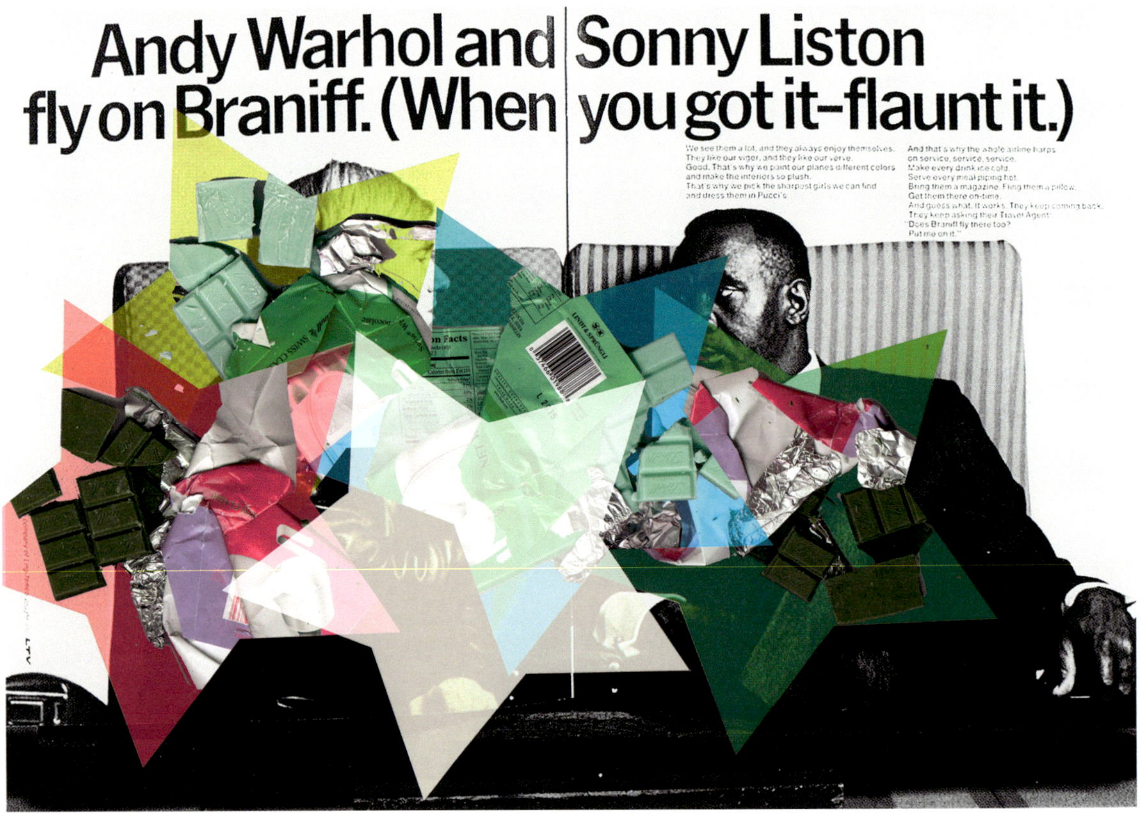
Andy Warhol and Sonny Liston fly on Braniff. (When you got it–flaunt it.)
We see them a lot, and they always enjoy themselves. They like our vigor, and they like our verve. Good. That's why we paint our planes different colors and make the interiors so plush. That's why we pick the sharpest girls we can find and dress them in Pucci's.
And that's why the whole airline harps on service, service, service. Make every drink ice cold. Serve every meal piping hot. Bring them a magazine. Fling them a pillow. Get them there on-time. And guess what. It works. They keep coming back. They keep asking their Travel Agent: "Does Braniff fly there too? Put me on it."

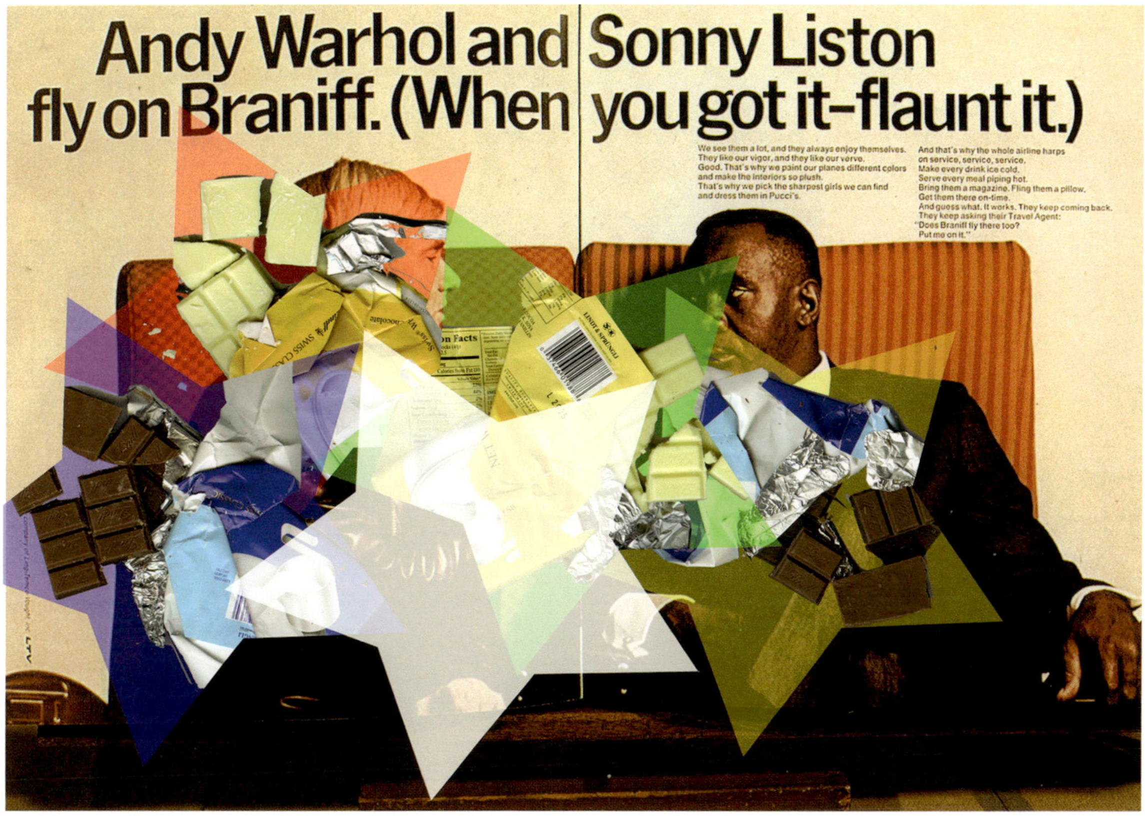
Andy Warhol and Sonny Liston fly on Braniff. (When you got it–flaunt it.)
We see them a lot, and they always enjoy themselves.
They like our vigor, and they like our verve.
Good. That's why we paint our planes different colors
and make the interiors so plush.
That's why we pick the sharpest girls we can find
and dress them in Pucci's.
And that's why the whole airline harps
on service, service, service.
Make every drink ice cold.
Serve every meal piping hot.
Bring them a magazine. Fling them a pillow.
Get them there on-time.
And guess what. It works. They keep coming back.
They keep asking their Travel Agent:
"Does Braniff fly there too?
Put me on it."

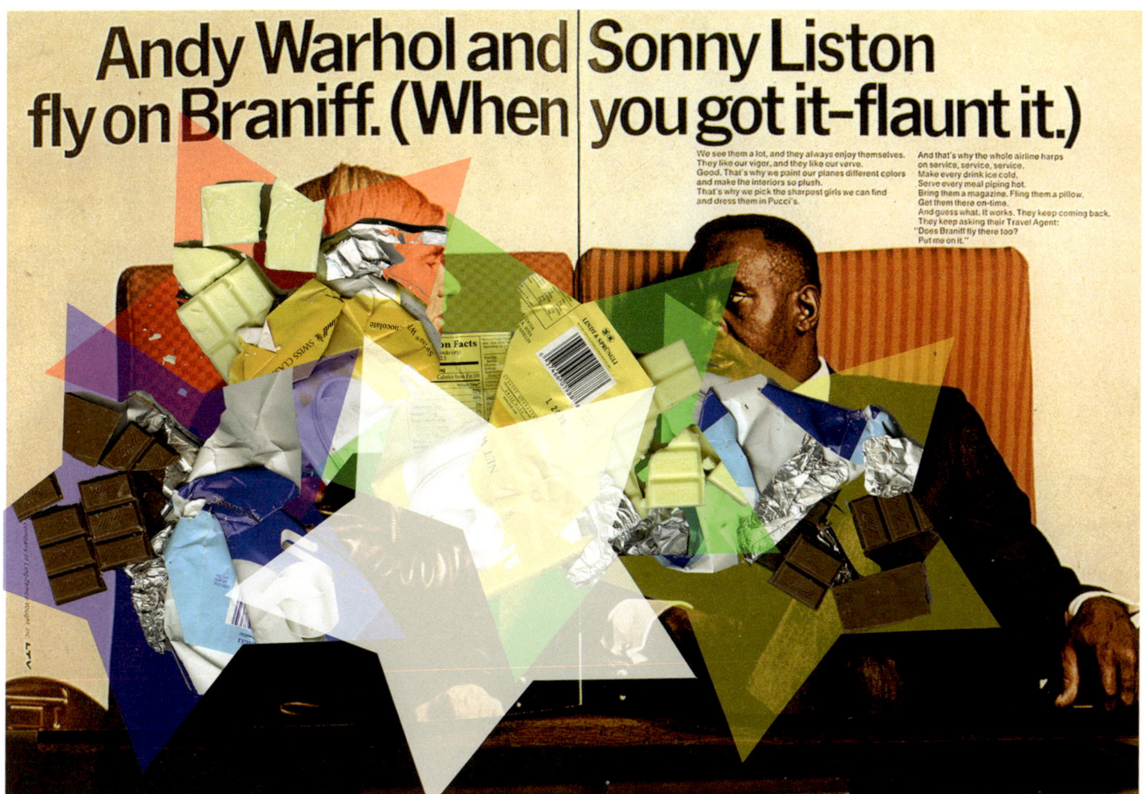
Andy Warhol and Sonny Liston fly on Braniff. (When you got it–flaunt it.)
We see them a lot, and they always enjoy themselves.
They like our vigor, and they like our verve.
Good. That's why we paint our planes different colors
and make the interiors so plush.
That's why we pick the sharpest girls we can find
and dress them in Pucci's.
And that's why the whole airline harps
on service, service, service.
Make every drink ice cold.
Serve every meal piping hot.
Bring them a magazine. Fling them a pillow.
Get them there on-time.
And guess what. It works. They keep coming back.
They keep asking their Travel Agent:
"Does Braniff fly there too?
Put me on it."

EXHIBITION CHECKLIST

Sean Dack (U.S., b. 1976)
Building (Sir Norman Foster). 2008
Chromogenic print
30 × 44 1/2 in.
Courtesy of the artist and Fredric Snitzer Gallery, Miami, Florida

Glitch Girl #4. 2008
Chromogenic print
44 1/2 × 30 in.
Courtesy of the artist and Fredric Snitzer Gallery, Miami, Florida

Wing (Economy Class). 2006
Chromogenic print
30 × 44 1/2 in.
Courtesy of the artist and Fredric Snitzer Gallery, Miami, Florida

Untitled (Beach). 2008
Chromogenic print
30 × 44 1/2 in.
Courtesy of the artist and Fredric Snitzer Gallery, Miami, Florida

Clouds. 2007
Chromogenic print
43 × 30 in.
Courtesy of the artist and Fredric Snitzer Gallery, Miami, Florida

Karl Haendel (U.S., b. 1976)
High Noon #2. 2008
Pencil on paper
90 × 78 in.
Collection of Helen and Charles Schwab

Walead #2. 2009
Pencil on paper
52 × 41 in.
Collection of the artist

Cracked Mirror #3. 2009
Pencil on paper with staples
82 × 45 in.
Courtesy of Yvon Lambert, Paris

Everything, Nothing, Something (after Emily Mast). 2009
Pencil on paper
30 × 22 in.
Courtesy of Susanne Vielmetter Los Angeles Projects

Power Cord (negative) #1. 2009
Pencil on paper
83 × 52 in.
Courtesy of Susanne Vielmetter Los Angeles Projects

Headlines #5. 2008
Pencil on paper
30 × 22 in.
Collection Robert Harshorn Shimshak and Marion Brenner

Lightning #28. 2009
Charcoal on paper
30 × 22 in.
Courtesy of Susanne Vielmetter Los Angeles Projects

Screaming Baby [negative]. 2007
Unique Chromogenic print
78 × 50 in.
Courtesy of the artist and Artist Pension Trust

Karl-o-gram #7. 2009
Pencil on paper
30 × 22 in.
Courtesy of Harris Lieberman Gallery, New York

Pencil Stubs #7. 2009
Pencil on paper
41 × 26 in.
Courtesy of Susanne Vielmetter Los Angeles Projects

Anitra's Dance. 2007
Pencil on paper
52 × 40 in.
Collection of the artist

Maltese Falcon. 2009
Pencil on paper on board
52 × 64 in.
Courtesy of Susanne Vielmetter Los Angeles Projects

Somewhat Cubist #15. 2009
Enamel on paper
52 × 72 in.
Courtesy of Susanne Vielmetter Los Angeles Projects

Jordan Kantor (U.S., b. 1972)
Untitled (eclipse). 2001
Transfer carbon on paper
32 3/16 × 23 in.
Private collection, San Francisco

Eclipse (color inversion). 2009
Oil on canvas
30 × 40 in.
Piper Family Collection

Eclipse. 2009
Five screenprints on clear polycarbonate and silver Mylar sheets
30 × 34 1/2 in. each
Courtesy of the artist and Ratio 3

Matt Keegan (U.S., b. 1976)
Images are Words/Las Imágenes son Palabras. 2010
Chromogenic prints, table with laminated images hand assembled by the artist's mother, two-channel video
Dimensions variable
Courtesy of the artist and Altman Siegel Gallery, San Francisco

Carter Mull (U.S., b. 1977)
Expenditure. 2010
Type-C print with pasted print
41 7/16 × 64 1/2 in.
Courtesy of the artist and Marc Foxx Gallery

Passenger. 2010
Type-C print with pasted print
41 7/16 × 64 1/2 in.
Courtesy of the artist and Marc Foxx Gallery

The Tar Pit. 2010
Type-C print with pasted print
41 7/16 × 64 1/2 in.
Courtesy of the artist and Marc Foxx Gallery

Horseradish, New York Times April 1, 2010.
2010
Ink on paper
16 3/4 × 21 3/4 in.
Courtesy of the artist and Marc Foxx Gallery

Lobby, New York Times April 20, 2010.
2010
Ink on paper
16 3/4 × 21 3/4 in.
Courtesy of the artist and Marc Foxx Gallery

Over (April 7, 2010). 2010
Ink on paper
16 5/8 × 21 3/4 in.
Courtesy of the artist and Marc Foxx Gallery

Spilling, New York Times May 7, 2010. 2010
Ink on paper
16 3/4 × 21 3/4 in.
Private Collection
Courtesy of the artist and Marc Foxx Gallery

Lisa Oppenheim (U.S., b. 1975)
No Closer to the Source (July 20, 1969). 2008
Double 16mm film projection
3:22
Courtesy of the artist and Harris Lieberman Gallery, New York
Henry Art Gallery venue only

The Sun is Always Setting Somewhere Else... 2006
35mm slide projection, 15 slides
Collection of Kelly and Jeff Poe, Santa Monica, CA
Courtesy of the artist and Harris Lieberman Gallery, New York

Marlo Pascual (U.S., b. 1972)
Untitled. 2009
Digital Chromogenic print, rock
10 × 30 3/4 × 21 in.
Private collection, promised gift to the Seattle Art Museum

Untitled. 2009
Digital Chromogenic print, wood
96 × 48 in.
Collection of Dr. Paul Marks, Toronto

Amanda Ross-Ho (U.S., b. 1975)
Camera 1, Camera 2. 2007
Digital Chromogenic prints
48 × 48 in. and 52 × 41 in.
Private Collection
Courtesy of Cherry and Martin, Los Angeles

Camera (Aerial View). 2008
Mirrored security dome, canvas on panel
66 × 48 × 18 in.
Courtesy of the artist and Artist Pension Trust

Camera (Aerial View). 2008
Mirrored security dome, canvas on panel
66 × 48 × 18 in.
Courtesy of Cherry and Martin, Los Angeles

Camera (Aerial View). 2008
Mirrored security dome, canvas on panel
66 × 48 × 18 in.
Courtesy of Cherry and Martin, Los Angeles

Camera (Aerial View). 2008
Mirrored security dome, canvas on panel
66 × 48 × 18 in.
Courtesy of Cherry and Martin, Los Angeles

Camera (Aerial View). 2008
Mirrored security dome, canvas on panel
66 × 48 × 18 in.
Courtesy of Cherry and Martin, Los Angeles

Camera (Aerial View). 2008
Mirrored security dome, canvas on panel
66 × 48 × 18 in.
Courtesy of Cherry and Martin, Los Angeles

Sara VanDerBeek (U.S., b. 1976)
Four Photographers. 2008
Six digital Chromogenic prints
18 × 21 in. each
Miller Meigs Collection
Courtesy of the artist and Altman Siegel Gallery, San Francisco and Metro Pictures, New York

Caryatid. 2010
Chromogenic print
74 × 48 in.
Courtesy of the artist and Altman Siegel Gallery, San Francisco and Metro Pictures, New York

Venus Inverse. 2010
Chromogenic print
60 × 38 in.
Courtesy of the artist and Altman Siegel Gallery, San Francisco and Metro Pictures, New York

Siebren Versteeg (U.S., b. 1971)
Untitled Film IV. 2007
PC, Internet-connected computer program, digital projector, real time random images from Flickr.com
Courtesy of the artist and Max Protetch Gallery

White Flag. 2010
Clay, fluorescent light, Giclée on cotton
96 × 12 × 12 in.
Courtesy of the artist and Max Protetch Gallery

White Flag. 2010
Clay, fluorescent light, Giclée on cotton
96 × 12 × 12 in.
Courtesy of the artist and Max Protetch Gallery

White Flag. 2010
Clay, fluorescent light, Giclée on cotton
96 × 12 × 12 in.
Courtesy of the artist and Max Protetch Gallery

Erika Vogt (U.S., b. 1973)
Motor Post Motor Band Disband. 2006-2008
Digital video, wooden stand, painted surface
22:00
Courtesy of the artist and Overduin and Kite

I arrive when I am foreign (Centennial Tin). 2006
Lightjet Type-C print
92 × 46 1/2 in.
Courtesy of the artist and Overduin and Kite

I arrive when I am foreign (Mid-century Plywood). 2006
Lightjet Type-C print
92 × 46 1/2 in.
Courtesy of the artist and Overduin and Kite

I arrive when I am foreign (Record No Record). 2007
Lightjet Type-C Prints
93 × 46 in. (each)
Collection of John Rubeli, Los Angeles
Courtesy of Overduin and Kite
Henry Art Gallery venue only

Kelley Walker (U.S., b. 1969)
Andy Warhol and Sonny Liston Fly on Braniff (When you got it-flaunt it). 2005-2007
3 offset color posters
40 × 28 in. each
©Kelley Walker. Courtesy of artist and Paula Cooper Gallery

Untitled. 2010
Four-color process silkscreen with acrylic ink on canvas, *Penthouse*; December 1973
60 × 48 in.
©Kelley Walker. Courtesy of artist and Paula Cooper Gallery
Henry Art Gallery venue only

Untitled. 2010
Four-color process silkscreen with acrylic ink on canvas, *Der Speigel*; 14 November 1977
96 × 16 in.
©Kelley Walker. Courtesy of artist and Paula Cooper Gallery
Henry Art Gallery venue only

Photography credits:
p. 35, 36: Photo: Jesse David Harris.
p. 62, 64–65, 66–67: Image courtesy of the artist and Casey Kaplan, New York. Photo: Cary Whittier.
p. 68, 71, 72–73: Photo: Robert Wedemeyer.

STAFF LIST

Eric Adami Preparator
Alexa Anderson Gallery Service Representative
Lisa Jo Anderson Human Resources Manager and Administrator
Merith Bennett Curatorial Associate
Betsey Brock Associate Director for Communications & Outreach
Elizabeth A. Brown Chief Curator and Director of Exhibitions & Collections
Paul Cabarga Exhibitions Manager
Eric Carson Visitor Services & Security Supervisor
Paula Castillo UW Custodial Services
Harold Churchill III Gallery Service Representative
Ella Dorband Gallery Service Representative
Whitney Ford-Terry Program Coordinator
Orlando Francisco Gallery Service Representative
Dan Gurney Supervising Preparator
Hannah Hong Gallery Service Representative
Jennifer King Bookkeeper
Sara Krajewski Associate Curator
Angela Lindou Grants & Sponsorships
Robyn MacIntire Director of Development
Robert Nicholl Gallery Service Representative
William Owen Gallery Service Representative
Max Pethe Temp Prep
Maria Reyna Visitor Services & Tour Coordinator
Bob Rini Gallery Service Representative
Jim Rittimann Head Preparator & Exhibition Designer
Kevin Rochat Gallery Service Representative
Owen Santos Operations Manager
Kathy Savory Senior Development Associate
David Smith System Administrator
Judy Sourakli Curator of Collections
Anne Walsh Director of Finance
Sylvia Wolf Director
Jayme Yen Graphic Designer